PRACTICE TEST I

1) when Inline editing updates the field?

A. The field is saved/updated

B. When the record is saved/updated

C. When the return key is pressed

D. None of the above

2) If a company chooses to utilize Custom Fiscal Years, they are unable to utilize the standard forecasting option.

A. True

B. False

3) Which of the following objects are not considered standard objects?

A. Opportunities

B. Solutions

C. Job Applicants

D. Accounts

E. Campaigns

4) Which of the following features are included in the Service Cloud offering? (choose 2 answers)

A. Opportunities

B. Knowledge

C. Entitlements

D. Campaigns

E. Quotes

5) Locale settings dictate how users perceive date formats, time formats, and number formats.

A. True

B. False

6) If the company's locale is set to US English, all users will be assigned a default locale of US English, which cannot be changed.

A. True

B. False

7) If your company's fiscal year aligns with the Gregorian calendar, you are required to use Custom Fiscal Years in Salesforce.

A. True

Salesforce ADM-201: Salesforce Certified Administrator

Exam Preparation

Achieve **success** in your **Salesforce ADM-201 Exam** on the **first try** with our **new** and **exclusive preparation book**.

This **New and Exclusive book** is **designed** to **help you test** your **knowledge**, **providing** a **collection** of the **latest questions** with **detailed explanations** and **official references**.

Save both **time** and **money** by **investing in this book**, which **covers all the topics included** in the **Salesforce ADM-201 exam**.

This book includes **two full-length, highly important practice tests, each** with **60 questions**, for a **total** of **120 questions**. It also provides **detailed explanations** for **each question** and **official reference links**.

Dedicate your **effort** to **mastering** these **Salesforce ADM-201 exam questions**, as they **offer up-to-date information** on the **entire exam syllabus**.

This book is **strategically crafted** to not only assess your **knowledge** and **skills** but also to **boost your confidence for the official exam**.

With a **focus** on **thorough preparation**, **passing** the **official Salesforce ADM-201 Exam** on your **first attempt becomes achievable** through **diligent study of these valuable resources**.

The **official exam** consists of **60 multiple-choice questions** and allows **105 minutes** for completion. A **passing score is 65%**, which translates to **39 correct answers**.

GEORGIODACCACHE

You have the **option** to **take the test** at a **testing center** or **remotely** using **your own computer.**

Welcome!

B. False

8) To activate the multi-currency feature in Salesforce, you must:

A. Contact Salesforce.com

B. Check the Enable Multi-currency checkbox in your Chatter profile.

C. Operate your business in at least two different countries.

D. You cannot enable this feature once you've implemented Salesforce.

9) Which feature effectively enables you to "lock" the converted amount on closed opportunities?

A. Locale

B. Company Profile

C. Multi-currency

D. Advanced Currency Management

E. None of the above

10) User interface settings are applied globally to all users in an org.

A. True

B. False

11) Which of the following statements are true regarding List Views?

A. Save list views for future use.

B. Specify which groups of users have access to the list view.

C. Print list views.

D. Follow records and view related Chatter posts.

E. Export List View data to Excel.

F. All of the above.

12) A _____ defines a collection of settings and permissions that determines what users can see in the user interface, and what they can do.

A. Role

B. Chatter feed

C. Profile

D. Company Profile

13) Which of the following is not considered a standard Profile? (choose 3 answers)

A. System Administrator.

B. Read only.

C. Marketing Director.

D. Partner Portal User.

E. Standard Administrator.

14) A user with a Chatter Free User profile can access records in Salesforce, such as Accounts and Contacts.

A. True

B. False

15) Permissions of standard profiles cannot be edited.

A. True

B. False

16) System administrators can adjust tab settings for custom profiles, including setting tabs as Default On, Default Off, or Hidden.

A. True

B. False

17) To prevent future access to the Salesforce org, the system administrator should take the following steps when a user leaves the company.

A. Delete their user record.

B. De-activate their user record.

C. Delete any accounts or contacts owned by that user.

D. None of the above.

18) A license is consumed by an active user record.

A. True

B. False

19) A system administrator can choose to block users from accessing the Salesforce org if they exceed a specified number of failed login attempts.

A. True

B. False

20) Where can a system administrator look to determine the reason why a user is unable to log in to Salesforce? (Select all that apply.)

A. The Login History related list on the user's record.

B. The user's profile.

C. Manage Users | Login History.

D. Call salesforce.com Support.

21) What should a system administrator utilize to deactivate an application for a group of users?

A. Sharing Rules

B. Web tabs

C. Page layouts

D. Profiles

E. Roles

22) To restrict a user from logging into the Salesforce org outside of normal business hours, the System Administrator would do this in:

A. The user record

B. The user's profile record

C. Network settings

D. The role hierarchy

E. None of the above

23) If a user attempts to log in from an IP address outside the range specified in their profile, what will happen?

A. They will be logged in as normal.

B. They will have to reset their password.

C. They will be prompted to activate their computer.

D. They will be denied access.

E. None of the above.

24) What occurs when a user logs in to Salesforce for the first time? (Select all that apply.)

A. A cookie is placed in the browser.

B. Pop ups are automatically disabled.

C. Their IP address is added to a trusted list.

D. They are prompted to answer a security question.

25) The system administrator needs to restrict tele sales teams from accessing Salesforce outside of the office. How can this be accomplished?

A. There is no way to do this.

B. Setup | Security Controls | Network Access and specify the team's range of IP addresses.

C. Add the range of IP addresses to the team's profile(s).

D. Contact salesforce.com as this feature must be enabled.

26) Permission sets can serve as an alternative to profiles.

A. True

B. False

27) A user can be assigned only one permission set.

A. True

B. False

28) This setting establishes the default access levels for users to records they do not own.

A. Organization Wide Defaults

B. Roles Hierarchy

C. Profiles

D. Sharing Rules

E. Manual Sharing

29) If a user has read-only access to records that they do not own, the following statements are true. (choose 3 answers)

A. The user can view the record but not edit it.

B. The user can view and delete the record, but not edit it.

C. The user can change the owner of the record.

D. The user can search for the record.

E. The user can report on the record.

30) To restrict view access to Account records for certain users in the organization, the OWD for Accounts should be set to:

A. Public Read Only

B. Public Read/Write/Transfer

C. Private

D. None of the above

31) In a private sharing model, which of the following can be utilized when Role Hierarchy alone is insufficient for granting record access to users? (choose 3 answers)

A. Forecasting

B. Sharing rules

C. Manual Sharing

D. Teams (Account, Sales and Case)

E. Apex Triggers

32) Criteria-based sharing rules enable administrators to share records based on field values instead of just relying on record ownership.

A. True

B. False

33) Public groups can simplify the creation of sharing rules for administrators.

A. True

B. False

34) Public groups can consist of any combination of other public groups, users, roles, and _____.

A. Profile

B. Roles & subordinates

C. Managers

D. None of the above

35) Sales reps at AW Computing require support from product managers for selling specific products. Product managers do not have access to Opportunities but need to obtain access when assisting with a particular deal. How can the system administrator accomplish this?

A. Notify the product manager using opportunity update reminders.

B. Use similar opportunities to show opportunities related to the product manager.

C. Enable account teams and allow users to add the product manager.

D. Enable sales teams and allow users to add the product manager.

36) Administrators can use manual sharing to grant one-time access to individual records, a capability not available to users even if they own the record.

A. True

B. False

37) Who has the ability to share records manually?

A. The record owner

B. The record owner's manager

C. The record owner's manager's manager

D. The system administrator

E. All of the above

F. None of the above

38) If Field Level Security restricts a user from viewing the Credit Card field on the Opportunity record, the user will also be restricted from seeing this field.

A. In a related list

B. In search results

C. In reports

D. In list views

E. All of the above

F. None of the above

39) A System Admin can perform the following actions on a standard field.

A. Change the field label

B. Add help text

C. Add/edit values of a picklist

D. Delete the field

E. All of the above

F. None of the above

40) Use a _____ picklist to filter the values of one picklist based on the value of another picklist.

A. Controlling

B. Multi-select

C. Dependent

D. Independent

41) A checkbox can serve as the controlling field for a dependent picklist.

A. True

B. False

42) AW Computing requires tracking of the manufacturer and model for specific computers and laptops. How can the system administrator ensure that the selection of a manufacturer influences the available values for the model?

A. Create a multi-select picklist field that includes both manufacturers and models.

B. Create a lookup field from the manufacturer object to the model object.

C. Create a manufacturer field as a controlling picklist and the model as a dependent picklist.

D. Create a manufacturer field as the dependent picklist and the model as the controlling picklist.

43) Lookup fields enable users to select a record from another object while entering data, establishing a parent-child relationship.

A. True

B. False

44) Which of the following statements are true regarding formula fields? (choose 3 answers)

A. They are read-only.

B. They will not display on record edit pages.

C. They will not display on record detail pages.

D. They are not searchable.

E. They will not display on reports.

45) A cross-object formula references fields from related parent objects.

A. True

B. False

46) Page layouts are assigned to _____.

A. Users

B. Profiles

C. Roles

D. Roles & subordinates

47) Use _____ to filter or segment picklist values based on the user's profile.

A. Record Types

B. User Profiles

C. Role Hierarchy

D. Business Processes

E. Field Level Security

48) Which of the following objects can utilize business processes? (choose 2 answers)

A. Cases

B. Opportunities

C. Campaigns

D. Knowledge

49) When creating a sales process, the System Administrator will be modifying/filtering the values of the _____ field.

A. Amount

B. Stage

C. Next Steps

D. Status

E. Close Date

50) The system administrator has been tasked with establishing a method for tracking product shipments to customers that is closely linked to the Opportunity record. Each Opportunity may have multiple associated shipment records, and it should be mandatory to associate a Shipment record with an Opportunity before saving it. The system administrator should create.

A. A cross object formula displaying Opportunity ID on the Shipment record.

B. A Master - Detail relationship on the Shipment object to the Opportunity object.

C. A lookup relationship on the Opportunity object to the Shipment object.

D. A lookup relationship with a lookup filter from Opportunity to Shipment.

51) To establish a many-to-many relationship between two objects, a junction object must be created. This junction object will have a Master-Detail relationship with both objects.

A. True

B. False

52) To activate Field History Tracking for an object, the system administrator must include the related list in the page layout.

A. True

B. False

53) To update records using the Data Loader, the CSV file must include a specific field.

A. Owner

B. Salesforce ID

C. Record Owner

D. Object Name

54) You will require a security token to access Salesforce via:

A. Import Wizard

B. Data Loader

C. Salesforce for Outlook

D. All of the above

55) The Data Loader can identify and handle duplicate records during the import process.

A. True

B. False

56) A system administrator can utilize the Import Wizard to import Opportunity records into Salesforce.

A. True

B. False

57) Before importing a set of records into Salesforce, what factors should a system administrator take into consideration? (choose 2 answers)

A. The import file should include a record owner for each record.

B. Validation rules are not triggered when importing data using the import wizard.

C. Data should be de-duplicated in the import file prior to import.

D. Currency field values will default to the personal currency of the record owner.

58) What options are available for creating a backup of data from Salesforce? (choose 3 answers)

A. Weekly Data Export

B. Data Loader

C. Import Wizard

D. Reports

E. Dashboards

59) Deleted records remain in the Recycle Bin for a maximum of 15 days.

A. True

B. False

60) Which report type offers a basic list of data without any subtotals?

A. Matrix

B. Summary

C. Tabular

D. Custom

E. Standard

ANSWERS AND EXPLANATIONS

1) The answer is A. The field is saved/updated.

Inline editing is designed to be efficient, so updates typically happen immediately without a separate save step.

Here's why the other options are incorrect:

B. When the record is saved/updated: This might be true for some implementations, but inline editing is specifically designed to update the field itself without needing to save the entire record.

C. When the return key is pressed: While pressing the return key might trigger saving the change in some applications, it's not universally true for inline editing. There could be other ways to confirm the update.

D. None of the above: As discussed earlier, option A accurately reflects the typical behavior of inline editing.

Inline editing is a feature of some software applications that allows users to edit the contents of a field or record directly within the application, rather than having to open a separate edit window or form. When a user makes changes to a field using inline editing, the changes are usually saved to the field automatically when the user leaves the field (e.g. by clicking outside the field or pressing the tab key).

2) A. True

Explanation: Salesforce does not allow the use of standard forecasting with Custom Fiscal Years. If Custom Fiscal Years are enabled, forecasting must be done using the Custom Fiscal Year settings.

After enabling custom fiscal years, when you define the first custom fiscal year, all existing forecasts, forecast history, and forecast adjustments from the first period of that year forward will be deleted.

3) C. Job Applicants is the correct answer, not a standard Salesforce object.

Here's the breakdown:

Opportunities, Accounts, Contacts, Leads, Cases, Tasks, and Events: These are all standard objects in Salesforce.

Job Applicants: Salesforce doesn't include a pre-built Job Applicants object for managing recruitment processes. Organizations might create a custom object for this purpose.

Therefore, C. Job Applicants is the non-standard object among the given options.

if you look in the schema builder solutions is listed under standard objects.

Solution is standard object:

https://developer.salesforce.com/docs/atlas.en-us.object_reference.meta/object_reference/sforce_api_objects_solution.htm

4) Out of the listed features, the ones included in the Service Cloud offering are:

B. Knowledge

C. Entitlements

Here's why:

Service Cloud focuses on providing excellent customer service.

Knowledge: This feature allows you to build a self-service knowledge base with articles, FAQs, and other resources that empower customers to find solutions independently.

Entitlements: This feature defines the level of service your customers are entitled to receive based on their contracts or service agreements. It helps streamline support processes and manage customer expectations.

On the other hand, the other options are more suited for different Salesforce clouds:

Opportunities (Sales Cloud): Manages sales pipeline and opportunities.

Campaigns (Marketing Cloud): Creates and manages marketing campaigns.

Quotes (Sales Cloud): Generates quotes for potential sales.

While some features might overlap between clouds, these options are primarily associated with other clouds within the Salesforce ecosystem.

Reference:

Knowledge is also part of the service clouds. It allows you to provide support, even self-support to your customers. Knowledge will have the articles and help resources needed to help resolve issues.

More info here:

https://help.salesforce.com/articleView?id=knowledge_whatis.htm&type=5

Entitlements determines the level of customer support that has been offered/setup and lets you manage this (it is part of the case management system).

You can find more info here:

https://help.salesforce.com/articleView?id=entitlements_parent_admin.htm&type=5

5) A. True

Explanation: Locale settings control the formatting of dates, times, and numbers to match the conventions of a specific region or language, affecting how users perceive and interpret these formats.

Locale settings play a crucial role in how users perceive various formats.

Here's how:

Date formats: Different regions have different ways of displaying dates. For example, the US might use MM/DD/YYYY (month/day/year), while Europe might use DD/MM/YYYY. Locale settings ensure dates are formatted according to the user's region.

Time formats: Similar to dates, time formats vary by region. A 12-hour clock with AM/PM is common in some areas, while a 24-hour clock is preferred in others. Locale settings adjust the time format based on user preference.

Number formats: Locale settings also dictate how numbers are displayed. For example, the US might use a comma for thousands of separators (1,000), while Europe might use a period (1.000). Locale settings ensure numbers are formatted according to user expectations.

By considering locale settings, applications can present information in a familiar and user-friendly way.

6) The answer is B. False.

While the company's default locale might be US English, it doesn't necessarily lock all users into that setting.

Here's why:

User Preferences: Many applications allow users to customize their locale settings, even if there's a company default. This enables users to see dates, times, and numbers in their preferred format based on their location.

System Settings: In some cases, user locale might be determined by system settings on the device being used to access the application.

Here are some scenarios to consider:

A company with a US English default locale might have employees working remotely from different countries. These employees could potentially change their individual locale settings to their preferred format.

If an application leverages the user's system settings, a user working in the US with a device set to a different locale might see information formatted differently from the company default.

Therefore, while the company's default locale can influence user experience, it's not necessarily a fixed setting for all users.

7) The answer is B. False.

If your company's fiscal year aligns with the Gregorian calendar, you are not required to use Custom Fiscal Years in Salesforce.

Here's why:

Standard Fiscal Year: Salesforce offers a Standard Fiscal Year option that follows the Gregorian calendar but allows you to choose any month as the starting point. For instance, you could have a fiscal year running from October 1st to September 30th, which still aligns with the Gregorian calendar but has a non-standard starting point.

Custom Fiscal Years: This option is for companies whose fiscal year structure deviates from the Gregorian calendar. Examples include fiscal years running from July to June or having quarters with unequal lengths.

So, if your fiscal year simply uses the Gregorian calendar with a custom starting month, you can leverage the standard fiscal year functionality in Salesforce. Custom Fiscal Years are only necessary for more complex fiscal year structures.

Reference:

https://help.salesforce.com/s/articleView?id=sf.setting_the_fiscal_year.htm&type=5

=> If your company follows the Gregorian calendar year but you want to change the fiscal year start month, use standard fiscal years. If your company does not observe a standard fiscal year, you can enable custom fiscal years, which define a more complex fiscal year structure.

8) The answer to activate the multi-currency feature in Salesforce is:

B. Check the Enable Multi-currency checkbox in your Setup.

Here's why the other options are incorrect:

A. Contact Salesforce.com: Enabling multi-currency is a configuration setting within Salesforce, not something that requires contacting Salesforce directly.

C. Operate your business in at least two different countries: While having a business with multiple currencies is a common use case for multi-currency, it's not a requirement for activating the feature.

D. You cannot enable this feature once you've implemented Salesforce: You can enable multi-currency at any point, even after initial Salesforce implementation.

To activate the multi-currency feature, you'll need administrative permissions in Salesforce.

Here's a quick guide:

Go to Setup.

In the Quick Find box, enter Company Information and select it.

Click Edit.

Under Currency Settings, select the Activate Multi-Currencies checkbox.

Click Save.

Once enabled, you can manage active currencies, set conversion rates, and configure other aspects of the multi-currency functionality.

9) Answer: D. Advanced Currency Management

Explanation: Advanced Currency Management in Salesforce allows you to "lock" the converted amount on closed opportunities, ensuring that the amount remains unchanged even if there are fluctuations in currency exchange rates.

Locale, Company Profile, and Multi-currency: These features don't directly address locking the converted amount. They focus on user preferences (Locale), general company information (Company Profile), and handling multiple currencies (Multi-currency).

Advanced Currency Management: This feature allows you to manage historical exchange rates. You can define dated exchange rates, meaning you can map a specific conversion rate to a particular date range. This way, once an opportunity closes on a specific date with a certain exchange rate, the converted amount remains locked using that rate even if the current exchange rate fluctuates.

So, Advanced Currency Management provides the functionality to "lock" the converted amount based on the exchange rate at the time of closing the opportunity.

Reference:

https://help.salesforce.com/s/articleView?id=sf.administration_about_advanced_currency_management.htm&type=5

10) A. True

Explanation: User interface settings, such as page layouts, theme settings, and related preferences, are applied globally to all users in a Salesforce org.

User interface settings in Salesforce can be applied both globally and to individual users, allowing for some level of customization within the organization.

User interface settings are global settings and determines how all users can view and access features on the user interface.

11) The correct answer is F. All of the above.

List views in Salesforce offer a variety of functionalities to manage and visualize your data:

Save list views for future use: You can create and save custom list views with specific filters and criteria to quickly access the data you need.

Specify which groups of users have access to the list view: Sharing settings allow you to control which users or groups can view a particular list view.

Print list views: You can generate printable versions of your list views for offline reference.

Export List View data to Excel: Data from list views can be exported to spreadsheets like Excel for further analysis or sharing.

Follow records and view related Chatter posts: While not directly within the list view itself, you can follow records displayed in the list view to stay updated on changes and access related Chatter posts for collaboration.

List views are a powerful tool for customizing how you see your data in Salesforce.

List Views in Salesforce allow users to save specific filters and column configurations for future use, specify which groups of users can access them, print the list view, follow records and view related Chatter posts, and export the list view data to Excel.

12) Answer: C. Profile

Explanation: A profile in Salesforce defines a collection of settings and permissions that control what users can see in the user interface and what they can do.

Here's a breakdown of why Profile is the better answer:

Profile: A profile in Salesforce defines a collection of settings and permissions that determine a user's access within the application. It includes:

Object-level permissions: These grant access to specific objects (like Accounts or Contacts) and control what actions users can perform (read, edit, create, etc.).

Field-level security: This allows you to restrict access to specific fields within an object, providing granular control over user visibility.

Default settings: These define user preferences like time zone, language, and currency.

Role: While roles also play a part in user permissions, they primarily focus on data visibility based on a hierarchical structure. Users inherit permissions from roles higher up in the hierarchy.

In essence, profiles define the core permissions and settings for a user, while roles can be used to layer on additional access controls based on user position within the organization.

13) Correct answer: BCE

B. Read only

C. Marketing Director

E. Standard Administrator

B. Read Only: While you can create a custom profile with read-only permissions for specific objects in Salesforce, it's not a pre-built standard profile. Standard profiles typically offer some level of Create, Edit, or Delete access.

C. Marketing Director: As you mentioned, this is more likely a custom profile tailored to the specific needs and permissions of marketing directors within your organization. Standard profiles are designed for general user types, not specific job titles.

E. Standard Administrator: There's no standard profile named "Standard Administrator" in Salesforce. The closest equivalent would be the System Administrator profile, which comes pre-built with extensive administrative permissions.

Therefore, Read Only (B), Marketing Director (C), and Standard Administrator (E) are all non-standard profiles. System Administrator (A) is a standard profile, and while Read-Only functionality can be achieved with a custom profile, it's not a standard profile option by default.

The standard Profiles in Salesforce are:

- System Administrator
- Standard User
- Read Only
- Solution Manager
- Marketing User
- Contract Manager
- Partner User
- High Volume Customer Portal
- High Volume Portal
- Customer Portal Manager
- Customer Portal User
- Chatter Only User
- Salesforce Platform User
- Work.com Only User

Reference:

https://help.salesforce.com/s/articleView?id=sf.standard_profiles.htm&type=5

14) The answer is B. False.

A user with a Chatter Free User profile cannot access records in Salesforce, such as Accounts and Contacts.

Here's why:

Chatter Free User: This is a special user license designed to allow people who don't have a full Salesforce license to participate in social collaboration through Chatter.

Limited Access: Chatter Free users can see other users' profiles, participate in groups and feeds, and collaborate on posts. However, they cannot access the core data within Salesforce objects like Accounts or Contacts.

If a user needs access to Salesforce data beyond Chatter functionalities, they would require a standard Salesforce user license.

Users with Chatter Free user profile can access standard chatter items such as people, profiles, groups and files BUT they cannot access any Salesforce objects or data such as Accounts and Contacts.

Reference:

https://help.salesforce.com/s/articleView?id=sf.standard_profiles.htm&type=5

15) The answer is A. True. Permissions of standard profiles cannot be edited directly.

Here's why:

Standard Profiles: These are pre-built profiles provided by Salesforce with predefined sets of permissions for common user types like System Administrator, Sales Representative, or Customer Service Representative.

Permissions Control: Standard profiles offer a balance between functionality and security. Editing these permissions could potentially lead to security vulnerabilities or disrupt intended user access.

However, there are workarounds if you need to customize access for specific users:

Clone a Standard Profile: You can create a custom profile by cloning a standard profile and then modifying the permissions to fit your specific needs. This allows you to grant or restrict access to objects and fields based on your requirements.

Permission Sets: These are permission bundles that can be layered on top of user profiles to grant additional access. This approach lets you provide granular control over user permissions without modifying the standard profiles themselves.

So, while you cannot directly edit permissions of standard profiles, you can achieve similar customization through profile cloning and permission sets.

Every org includes standard profiles. In Professional, Enterprise, Unlimited, Performance, and Developer Editions, you can use standard profiles or create, edit, and delete custom profiles. In orgs where you can't create custom profiles (such as Contact Manager and Group Editions), you can assign standard profiles to your users, but you can't view or edit them.

While you can't edit standard profile permissions, you can edit the following settings

- Custom App Settings.
- Tab Settings.
- Desktop Integration Clients options.
- Session Settings.
- Password Policies.

Reference:

https://help.salesforce.com/articleView?id=standard_profiles.htm&type=5

16) A. True

Explanation: System administrators in Salesforce have the ability to customize tab settings for custom profiles, allowing them to specify whether tabs are Default On, Default Off, or Hidden for users assigned to those profiles.

System administrators can adjust tab settings for custom profiles in Salesforce. These settings determine which tabs are visible to users with that profile and how they are displayed.

Here's a breakdown of the options:

Default On: Tabs set to "Default On" will be visible by default when a user with that profile logs in.

Default Off: Tabs set to "Default Off" will be hidden by default, but users can still access them through the "All Tabs" menu.

Hidden: Tabs marked as "Hidden" are completely invisible to users with that profile and cannot be accessed through any menus.

By adjusting these settings, system administrators can control the user interface for different profiles within Salesforce. This allows them to customize the information displayed to users based on their roles and responsibilities.

For example, a Sales Representative profile might have the "Opportunities" tab set to "Default On" since it's a core aspect of their job. On the other hand, the "Campaigns" tab might be set to "Default Off" if it's not directly relevant to their daily tasks but can still be accessed if needed.

17) Answer: B. De-activate their user record

Explanation: It is recommended to de-activate the user's record to prevent future access to the Salesforce org. Deleting the user record or any accounts/contacts owned by the user may not be necessary or appropriate in all cases.

Data Integrity: Deleting the user record entirely can cause issues with data integrity and audit trails. Historical data owned by that user might be lost or become difficult to track.

Deactivating the User Record: This is the recommended approach. It ensures the user's login is disabled, preventing unauthorized access. However, the user record and its associated data are still preserved for future reference or reporting purposes.

Here are some additional steps a system administrator might consider:

C. Delete any accounts or contacts owned by the user (Optional): If the data is no longer required and there's no need to track ownership history, you can consider deleting accounts or contacts owned by the departing user. However, proceed with caution to avoid potential data loss.

Transfer ownership of records: Assigning ownership of the user's accounts, contacts, or other records to an active user can ensure data remains accessible and managed within the organization.

In conclusion, deactivating the user record (B) is the primary step to prevent unauthorized access, while data deletion (C) should be a separate consideration based on your specific needs.

You cannot delete users from Salesforce. You can remove their license or deactivate them to remove their access to the system.

Reference:

https://admin.salesforce.com/blog/2015/users-may-come-go-records-must-live

18) A. True

Explanation: In Salesforce, each active user record consumes a user license, which determines the user's access and capabilities within the org.

A license is consumed by an active user record in Salesforce.

Here's why:

Salesforce Licenses: These licenses grant users access to the Salesforce platform and its functionalities. Organizations purchase a certain number of licenses based on their user base.

Active User Record: When a user has an active record in Salesforce and is assigned a user license, it counts towards the total number of licenses being consumed by the organization.

There are two main types of user licenses in Salesforce:

User Licenses: These are the core licenses that determine the baseline level of access a user has within the platform.

Permission Set Licenses: These are optional licenses that grant additional functionality beyond a user's base profile permissions.

Both user licenses and permission set licenses contribute to the total number of licenses being consumed, as long as they are assigned to active user records.

19) A. True

Explanation: In Salesforce, system administrators have the ability to configure the security settings to lock out users who exceed a certain number of failed login attempts, helping to protect the org from unauthorized access.

Salesforce provides security features that allow system administrators to block users from accessing the organization after exceeding a specified number of failed login attempts.

Here's why:

Password Policy Settings: Within Salesforce settings, administrators can configure password policies. These policies include defining:

Minimum password length

Password complexity requirements (uppercase letters, lowercase letters, numbers, symbols)

Maximum number of failed logins attempts before lockout

Lockout Mechanism: If a user exceeds the defined number of failed attempts, their account gets locked for a specific period. This helps prevent unauthorized access attempts through brute-force methods.

So, system administrators have the ability to configure password policies that include lockout mechanisms based on failed login attempts.

Reference:

https://help.salesforce.com/s/articleView?id=sf.users_login_history.htm&type=5

=> As an admin, you can monitor all login attempts to Salesforce, to your Experience Cloud sites, and to logins to connected apps that use insecure flows.

20) Correct answer: AC

A. The Login History related list on the user's record.

C. Manage Users | Login History.

These options provide information directly related to login attempts, including success/failure status, timestamps, and potentially the reason for failure (e.g., exceeded attempts, invalid credentials).

While Salesforce support (D) can be a resource, it's recommended to check the login history first for a more immediate diagnosis. User profiles (B) focus on permissions and access control, not login functionality itself.

Here's a breakdown of all the options:

A. The Login History related list on the user's record: This list offers specific details about the user's login attempts, making it a valuable first step.

B. The user's profile: While a deactivated profile might prevent login, the login history provides more focused information on the login attempt itself.

C. Manage Users | Login History: This broader view of login history across the organization allows filtering by user or date range for a wider perspective.

D. Call Salesforce.com Support: This can be helpful for complex issues, but it's recommended to check the login history first for a quicker resolution.

You can test it:

1- Setup > Users > user record > Login History

2- Setup > Setup > Login History

21) Answer: D. Profiles

Explanation: Profiles in Salesforce control which applications and features users can access. By modifying the permissions in a profile, a system administrator can deactivate an application for a group of users.

Profiles: Profiles in Salesforce define a collection of settings and permissions that control what users can see and do within the application. This includes object-level permissions that grant access to specific objects (like Accounts or Contacts) and the ability to perform actions like creating, editing, or deleting them.

Sharing Rules: These are used to share data with specific users or groups, not to deactivate applications entirely.

Web Tabs: These are custom tabs that link to external websites or applications. They don't directly control access to applications within Salesforce.

Page Layouts: These define how fields are arranged on record detail pages. They don't affect application access at the user level.

Roles: While roles can be used in conjunction with profiles for permission inheritance, profiles provide the core mechanism for controlling application access through object-level permissions.

By editing the profiles assigned to a group of users, a system administrator can remove the "Visible" checkbox for the unwanted application. This effectively deactivates the application for those users, preventing them from seeing or using it within Salesforce.

Disable a Custom App in a Profile:

---

1. Click the gear icon then go to Setup | Administration | Users | Profiles.

2. Look for the Profile you want to modify.

3. Click Edit.

4. Under "Custom App Settings" uncheck the Visible checkbox to disable the App.

5. Click Save.

Disable a Custom App in the App itself:

---

1. Click the gear icon then go to Setup | Apps | App Manager.

2. Click the drop down then click Edit on the App you want to remove the Profile from.

3. Select User Profiles under App Settings.

4. Under Selected Profiles, click the Profile then click the Remove icon.

5. Click Save.

Reference:

https://help.salesforce.com/s/articleView?id=000385899&type=1

22) The answer to restrict a user from logging into Salesforce outside of business hours is:

B. The user's profile record

Here's why:

User Profiles: These define a collection of settings and permissions for users in Salesforce. One of the configurable settings within a profile is Login Hours.

Login Hours: This feature allows you to specify the days and times when users with that profile can log in to the Salesforce organization. You can set start and end times for each day, effectively restricting access outside of designated business hours.

Here's why the other options wouldn't work for this purpose:

A. The user record: While user records store various details, login hour restrictions are typically configured within the user's profile, which defines broader access settings.

C. Network settings: Network settings are typically managed by the IT department and control network-wide access, not user-specific login restrictions within Salesforce itself.

D. The role hierarchy: While roles can be used for permission inheritance within profiles, login hours are a setting within individual profiles, not something directly managed by the role hierarchy.

E. None of the above: Since Salesforce profiles offer Login Hours functionality, this is the most suitable option for restricting login based on time.

Reference:

https://trailhead.salesforce.com/content/learn/projects/protect-your-data-in-salesforce/restrict-login-hours-and-ip-ranges

23) Answer: D. They will be denied access.

Explanation: Salesforce's IP range restrictions are designed to enhance security by limiting access to specified IP addresses or ranges. If a user tries to log in from an IP address outside of the allowed range, they will be denied access for security reasons.

Login IP Ranges: Salesforce allows administrators to configure login IP ranges within user profiles. This acts as a security measure to restrict access only to authorized IP addresses.

Access Denial: If a user attempts to log in from an IP outside the allowed range, their login attempt will be denied. This helps prevent unauthorized access attempts from unrecognized locations.

Here's why the other options are less likely:

A. They will be logged in as normal: This wouldn't be secure if the IP address is outside the authorized range.

B. They will have to reset their password: While a failed login attempt might trigger a notification or temporary lockout depending on security settings, a password reset wouldn't be the automatic response for an out-of-range IP.

C. They will be prompted to activate their computer: This doesn't apply to Salesforce logins. It might be relevant for software activation on a personal device.

E. None of the above: Denial of access (D) is the most likely outcome based on the functionality of Login IP Ranges in Salesforce profiles.

Reference:

https://help.salesforce.com/s/articleView?id=000386441&type=1

=> Users will not be able to access Salesforce from any IP that is not listed in the range. They will receive a Restricted IP error when logging in.

24) There are two options out of the provided ones that occur when a user logs in to Salesforce for the first time:

A. A cookie is placed in the browser.

D. They are prompted to answer a security question.

Here's why:

A. Cookies: When a user logs in, Salesforce typically creates a session cookie in their browser. This cookie helps maintain the login session and identify the user throughout their browsing activity within Salesforce.

D. Security Question: As part of the initial login setup, users are often prompted to create a security question and answer. This information can be used to verify their identity if they forget their password in the future.

Here's why the other options are less likely:

B. Pop ups are automatically disabled: Salesforce doesn't automatically disable pop-ups for users.

C. Their IP address is added to a trusted list: While IP address information might be logged during login, there's no automatic addition to a trusted list based solely on the first login. Login IP ranges can be configured in user profiles for security purposes, but that's a separate configuration.

25) C. Add the range of IP addresses to the team's profile(s)

Adding the range of IP addresses to the team's profiles means that users assigned to those profiles will only be able to access Salesforce from IP addresses within the specified range. This helps restrict access to Salesforce for the tele sales teams to only when they are in the office, as access from outside the specified IP range will be denied.

Reference:

Profiles

=> https://help.salesforce.com/s/articleView?id=sf.login_ip_ranges.htm&type=5

=> https://help.salesforce.com/s/articleView?id=sf.security_networkaccess.htm&type=5

To help protect your organization's data from unauthorized access, you can specify a list of IP addresses from which users can log in without receiving a login challenge. However, this does not restrict access, entirely, for users outside of the Trusted IP

Range. After these users complete the login challenge (usually by entering a code sent to their mobile device or email address), they can log in.

26) B. False

Profiles: These are the essential foundation of user access control in Salesforce. They define a collection of standard permissions for various user types, granting them basic functionalities within the application (e.g., creating and editing accounts, managing opportunities).

Permission Sets: These are collections of additional permissions that can be assigned to user profiles. They provide a way to extend a user's access beyond the baseline permissions defined in their profile.

Why Permission Sets Aren't a Full Replacement:

Core Permissions: Profiles provide the core set of permissions that most users will need to perform their basic tasks within Salesforce. Permission sets cannot entirely replace this foundation.

User Assignment: Every user must be assigned a profile, while permission sets are optional additions.

How Permission Sets Work as an Extension:

Customization: Permission sets offer a way to customize user access for specific needs. If a user requires additional permissions beyond their profile's defaults, a permission set can be created and assigned to grant those extra functionalities.

Granular Control: They allow for more granular control compared to profiles. You can assign multiple permission sets to a single user, combining permissions from various sets to create a tailored access experience.

In essence, permission sets are powerful tools for extending and customizing user access, but they cannot entirely replace profiles as the core foundation of user permissions in Salesforce.

Essentially, a user's profile is the baseline authorization of access to the Org. Permission sets are, as the name implies, a set of additional CRED permissions that can be applied to different profiles. Typically, they are task-based and related to different Objects and managed packages.

27) The answer is B. False.

A user in Salesforce can be assigned multiple permission sets in addition to their assigned profile.

Here's why:

Profiles: These define the baseline permissions for a user.

Permission Sets: These are collections of additional permissions that can be layered on top of a user profile.

By assigning multiple permission sets to a user, you can grant them a combination of specific permissions beyond their profile's base functionalities. This allows for more granular control over user access within Salesforce.

=> https://help.salesforce.com/s/articleView?id=sf.perm_sets_overview.htm&type=5

Users can have only one profile but, depending on the Salesforce edition, they can have multiple permission sets. You can assign permission sets to various types of users, regardless of their profiles.

28) Answer: A. Organization Wide Defaults

Explanation: Organization Wide Defaults (OWD) in Salesforce determine the default level of access that all users have to records they do not own. This setting is the foundation for sharing settings in Salesforce.

Organization Wide Defaults (OWD): This setting defines the base level of access that all users have to specific object types (e.g., Accounts, Contacts, Opportunities) when they don't own the record. It determines whether users can view only (Read), view and edit (Read/Write), or have full access (Read/Write/Transfer) to these records by default.

Here's how the other options influence access control:

B. Roles Hierarchy: This defines a structure where users inherit permissions from higher-level roles. While it can influence access, it doesn't directly set the default access level for all users.

C. Profiles: Profiles define a collection of permissions for user types. They can include sharing settings that influence record access, but OWD sets the baseline for everyone.

D. Sharing Rules: These are more specific rules that grant or restrict access to individual records or groups of records based on criteria like owner, record type, or field values. They are layered on top of the OWD settings.

E. Manual Sharing: This allows users to manually share individual records with other users, granting specific access levels. It provides granular control but doesn't define the default for all users.

In summary, Organization Wide Defaults (OWD) is the primary mechanism for setting the baseline access level for users to records they don't own in Salesforce.

Answer is A because it says "default levels of access" -- which are controlled by OWD only.

Reference:

https://help.salesforce.com/s/articleView?id=sf.security_data_access.htm&type=5

Organization-wide sharing settings:

Organization-wide sharing settings specify the default level of access that users have to each other's records.

29) Correct answer: ADE

A. The user can view the record but not edit it.

D. The user can search for the record.

E. The user can report on the record.

Explanation: With read-only access, the user can view the record but cannot edit it. They can search for the record and include it in reports, but they cannot delete it or change its owner.

A. The user can view the record but not edit it. This is the core limitation of read-only access. Users can see the information in the record but cannot modify any of the fields.

D. The user can search for the record. As long as the record meets the search criteria and the user has the appropriate object-level permission to view that type of record (e.g., Accounts or Contacts), they should be able to find it through a search.

E. The user can report on the record. Just like searching, if the user has the necessary object-level permission, they should be able to include the record in reports, allowing them to analyze the data within the record.

Let's explore why the other statements are not true:

B. The user can view and delete the record, but not edit it: Deleting records is typically a restricted action, often requiring additional permissions beyond read-only access.

C. The user can change the owner of the record: Changing ownership is another action that usually requires higher-level permissions than read-only access.

Reference:

https://help.salesforce.com/s/articleView?id=sf.sharing_model_fields.htm&type=5

Public Read Only

All users can view and report on records but not edit them. Only the owner, and users above that role in the hierarchy, can edit those records.

30) The best option to restrict view access to Account records for certain users in Salesforce is:

C. Private

Here's why:

Organization Wide Defaults (OWD): This setting defines the baseline access level that all users have for specific object types (like Accounts) when they don't own the record.

Private: By setting the OWD for Accounts to Private, the default access level becomes "no access" for all users. This means users will not be able to view Account records by default unless additional sharing rules or manual sharing is implemented to grant them access.

Here's why the other options wouldn't achieve the desired restriction:

A. Public Read Only: This would allow users to see Account records, which is the opposite of restricting view access.

B. Public Read/Write/Transfer: This grants extensive access, including viewing, editing, and even transferring ownership of Account records, which is far beyond restricting view access.

D. None of the Above: While there might be other ways to restrict access (sharing rules, permission sets), setting the OWD to Private is a direct and effective approach to establish the baseline restriction.

Additional Considerations:

After setting the OWD to Private, you can define specific sharing rules to grant read access (or even edit access) to specific users or groups who need it.

Manually sharing Account records with individual users is another option for granting access beyond the OWD.

Reference:

https://help.salesforce.com/s/articleView?id=sf.security_sharing_owd_users.htm&type=5

For user records, you can set the organization-wide sharing default to Private or Public Read Only. The default must be set to Private if there is at least one user who shouldn't see a record.

31) In a private sharing model, the following can be utilized when Role Hierarchy alone is insufficient for granting record access to users:

B. Sharing rules: Sharing rules are used to extend sharing access to users in public groups or roles.

C. Manual Sharing: Allows record owners or users with the "Modify All" permission to share individual records with other users or groups.

D. Teams (Account, Sales and Case): Teams allow for additional grouping of users beyond the role hierarchy to provide access to records.

Explanation:

Forecasting (A) is not directly related to record access in Salesforce.

Apex Triggers (E) can be used to automate processes in Salesforce but are not specific to record sharing.

Reference:

https://help.salesforce.com/s/articleView?id=sf.managing_the_sharing_model.htm&type=5

*** Teams is another Method for Controlling Access to Records.

32) A. True

Explanation: Criteria-based sharing rules in Salesforce allow administrators to define criteria based on field values to share records with specific users or groups, providing more granular control over record access beyond just ownership.

A criteria-based sharing rule determines with whom to share records based on field values. For example, you have a custom object for job applications, with a custom picklist field named "Department." A criteria-based sharing rule could share all job applications in which the Department field is set to "IT" with all IT managers in your organization.

Reference:

https://help.salesforce.com/s/articleView?id=sf.security_sharing_rule_types.htm&type=5

A criteria-based sharing rule determines with whom to share records based on field values.

A criteria-based sharing rule is based on record values and not the record owners.

33) A. True

Explanation: Public groups in Salesforce can be used in sharing rules to grant access to records, making it easier for administrators to manage and apply sharing settings to multiple users at once.

Public groups are indeed designed to simplify sharing rule

creation for administrators.

Here's why:

Sharing rules can grant access to users based on individual users, roles, or groups.

Public groups act as pre-defined collections of users, roles, or even other public groups.

By creating public groups that represent specific user needs, administrators can easily include those groups within sharing rules. This saves time and effort compared to manually adding individual users or roles each time.

Reference:

https://trailhead.salesforce.com/content/learn/modules/data_security/data_security_sharing_rules

A public group is an admin-defined grouping of users that can be used to simplify the creation of sharing rules.

34) B. Roles & subordinates

Explanation: Public groups in Salesforce can be composed of other public groups, individual users, roles, and their subordinates, allowing for flexible and dynamic grouping of users for sharing and collaboration purposes.

Incorrect options:

Profiles don't directly relate to sharing access.

Managers are users who hold specific roles, so they'd be included through the "users" or "roles" options.

Reference:

https://trailhead.salesforce.com/content/learn/modules/data_security/data_security_sharing_rules

Depending on the group member types available in your org, public groups can be a combination of:

- individual users.
- roles.
- roles and subordinates.
- territories.
- territories and subordinates.
- other public groups.

35) D. Enable sales teams and allow users to add the product manager.

While both Account Teams and Sales Teams can be used for sharing access, Sales Teams are indeed more relevant in this scenario.

Here's the breakdown:

Account Teams: Connect users to Accounts, which can be helpful if the product decision hinges on the specific account. However, opportunities are not directly tied to account teams.

Sales Teams: Connect users to Opportunities, which is exactly what the product managers need for this situation.

Therefore, enabling Sales Teams and allowing users to add the product manager is the most appropriate solution (choice D).

Enable Sales Team is correct because they are dealing with Opportunities.

Salesforce also has Opportunity Teams. Like Account Teams, these include a group of people who contribute in specific roles. However, they give access to different levels of data. Account Teams can have access to all the information on an account, like related contacts, cases, and opportunities. Your Salesforce admin can set the organization-wide defaults for accounts and opportunities to Private. In that case, if you give other users access to an individual opportunity, those users gain read-only access to the opportunity's primary account.

Reference:

https://trailhead.salesforce.com/it/content/learn/modules/sales-team-collaboration/sell-as-a-team

36) B. False

In Salesforce, record owners can grant one-time access to their records through manual sharing.

Here's the correction:

Both Record Owners and Administrators: Can grant one-time access to individual records through manual sharing. This provides flexibility for sharing data with specific users who need temporary access.

Here's why the statement is wrong:

Sharing settings and org-wide defaults might restrict the types of access a record owner can grant, but it doesn't necessarily prevent them from granting one-time access altogether.

Manual Sharing is used to grant one-off access. Manual sharing can be granted by the record owner, anyone above the owner in role hierarchy and System Administrator. Manual sharing is used to handle exception cases where access to a particular record needs to be given to a specific user. There is a Sharing button on the records page. This is used to provide manual sharing.

Reference:

https://help.salesforce.com/s/articleView?id=sf.granting_access_to_records.htm&type=5

Sometimes, granting access to one record includes access to all its associated records. For example, if you grant another user access to an account, the user automatically has access to all the opportunities and cases associated with that account.

To grant access to a record, you must be one of the following users.

The record owner.

A user in a role above the owner in the hierarchy (if your organization's sharing settings control access through hierarchies)

Any user granted Full Access to the record.

37) The answer is E. All of the above.

In Salesforce, several users can share records manually:

A. The record owner: They have the most basic level of control and can share the record with others depending on sharing settings and org defaults.

D. The system administrator: They have the highest level of control and can bypass sharing settings to grant access to any user or group.

B. The record owner's manager (and potentially higher managers): If the manager has a role in the hierarchy above the record owner, they might have permission to share the record based on the role hierarchy settings.

So, all of the options (A, B, C, and D) can potentially have the ability to share records manually depending on their specific permissions.

Reference:

https://help.salesforce.com/s/articleView?id=sf.granting_access_to_records.htm&type=5

Sometimes, granting access to one record includes access to all its associated records. For example, if you grant another user access to an account, the user automatically has access to all the opportunities and cases associated with that account.

To grant access to a record, you must be one of the following users.

The record owner.

A user in a role above the owner in the hierarchy (if your organization's sharing settings control access through hierarchies)

Any user granted Full Access to the record.

An administrator.

38) E. All of the above

Explanation: Field Level Security restrictions apply to all ways in which the field is presented, including related lists, search results, reports, and list views. If a user is restricted from viewing a field, they will not be able to see it in any of these contexts.

Field-Level Security controls a user's access to a specific field across the entire Salesforce platform. If a user is restricted from viewing the Credit Card field on the Opportunity record, this restriction applies to:

A. Related lists: If the Credit Card field is on a related list (e.g., Payments on the Opportunity), the user won't see it.

B. Search results: Search results include data from the restricted field, so the user won't see the credit card information.

C. Reports: Reports can display data from most fields, so the Credit Card field would be hidden if the user doesn't have access.

D. List views: List views of Opportunities can include various fields. If Credit Card is restricted, it won't be displayed in the list view.

Therefore, Field-Level Security has a comprehensive impact, restricting access to the field regardless of where the data appears within Salesforce.

Reference:

https://trailhead.salesforce.com/content/learn/modules/data_security/data_security_fields

Unlike page layouts, which only control the visibility of fields on detail and edit pages, field-level security controls the visibility of fields in any part of the app, including related lists, list views, reports, and search results. In fact, to make absolutely sure that a user can't access a particular field, it's important to use the field-level security page for a given object to restrict access to the field. There are simply no other shortcuts that provide the same level of protection for a particular field.

39) Correct answer: ABC

A. Change the field label

B. Add help text

C. Add/edit values of a picklist

Explanation: A System Admin can change the field label, add help text, and add or edit values of a picklist for a standard field in Salesforce. However, deleting a standard field is not possible; standard fields cannot be deleted, only hidden from users if they are not needed.

Standard fields are default fields built-in to Salesforce. They cannot be deleted. On the other hand, several aspects of standard fields can be customized as follows: Edit, delete, or add values in picklist fields and set a default value.

Reference:

You can change the name of almost any object, field, or tab in Salesforce.

For example, you can change the name label for the "Accounts" object and related "Accounts" tab to "Companies", and change the field "Account Name" to "Company Name."

https://help.salesforce.com/articleView?id=customize_rename.htm&type=5

40) The answer is C. Dependent.

A dependent picklist is a type of picklist where the available options in the second picklist depend on the selection made in the first picklist.

Here's how it works:

You have two picklist fields (let's call them Picklist 1 and Picklist 2).

Picklist 1 has various options.

Picklist 2 is initially blank or has limited generic options.

When a user selects a value in Picklist 1, the options in Picklist 2 dynamically update to show only the relevant choices based on the selection in Picklist 1.

This helps ensure data accuracy and streamlines data entry by guiding users towards the appropriate choices.

Dependent picklists in Salesforce allow you to define a relationship between two picklist fields where the values available in the dependent picklist are determined by the value selected in the controlling picklist. This helps to streamline data entry and ensure data accuracy.

Reference:

https://trailhead.salesforce.com/content/learn/modules/picklist_admin/picklist_admin_start

A dependent picklist filters values for one picklist based on a selection from another picklist or a checkbox (the controlling value) on the same record.

41) A. True

Explanation: In Salesforce, a checkbox can indeed serve as the controlling field for a dependent picklist. The values available in the dependent picklist can be controlled based on whether the checkbox is checked or unchecked.

Reference:

https://help.salesforce.com/s/articleView?id=sf.fields_about_dependent_fields.htm&type=5

A dependent picklist is a custom or multi-select picklist for which the valid values depend on the value of another field, called the controlling field. Controlling fields can be any picklist (with at least one and fewer than 300 values) or checkbox field on the same record.

42) The best way for the system administrator to achieve the desired functionality is:

C. Create a manufacturer field as a controlling picklist and the model as a dependent picklist.

By creating a controlling picklist field for the manufacturer and a dependent picklist field for the model, the system administrator can ensure that the selection of a manufacturer influences the available values for the model. This setup allows for a dynamic relationship between the two fields, where the available models are filtered based on the selected manufacturer.

Here's why this approach works:

Dependent picklists: These dynamically filter the available options based on the selection in the controlling field.

Manufacturer as controlling picklist: Selecting a specific manufacturer in this picklist will trigger the update of the model picklist.

Model as dependent picklist: This picklist will only show models associated with the chosen manufacturer, ensuring data accuracy and streamlining data entry.

The other options wouldn't achieve the same result:

A. Multi-select picklist: This wouldn't allow filtering based on the manufacturer selection. Users could potentially choose a model incompatible with the manufacturer.

B. Lookup field: Lookup fields connect records between objects, but they wouldn't provide the dynamic filtering needed to restrict model options based on the manufacturer.

D. Flipping controlling and dependent picklists: This would have the opposite effect. Choosing a model wouldn't restrict the manufacturer options.

Therefore, using a controlling picklist for the manufacturer and a dependent picklist for the model provides the ideal solution for AW Computing's requirement.

Create a manufacturer field as a controlling picklist and the model as a dependent picklist.

"a dependent picklist is a custom or multi-select picklist for which the valid values depend on the value of another field, called the controlling field".

43) A. True

Lookup fields are a valuable tool in Salesforce for creating relationships between records in different objects. Here's how they work:

Connecting Objects: A lookup field in one object points to a specific record in another object.

Data Selection: When users enter data, they can choose a record from the related object through a lookup window or search.

Relationship Types: Lookup fields don't inherently create a parent-child hierarchy, but they can establish master-detail or hierarchical relationships depending on how they're configured.

So, lookup fields do indeed enable users to select records and establish connections between objects in Salesforce.

In Salesforce, a lookup relationship is a type of child-to-parent relationship that allows you to relate one object to another object.

Despite having no impact on deletion or security, this kind of relationship connects two objects. Lookup fields are not necessarily required, unlike master-detail fields.

A parent-child relationship is not the same as a master-detail relationship. A lookup relationship always references a parent record.

44) Correct answer: ABD

A. They are read-only

B. They will not display on record edit pages

D. They are not searchable

Explanation:

Formula fields are read-only and their values are calculated based on other fields or values.

Formula fields are not displayed on record edit pages because they are calculated values.

Formula fields are not directly searchable in Salesforce, but their values can be used in filters and search criteria.

NOTE: Because formula fields are automatically calculated, they are read-only on record detail pages and do not update last modified date fields. Formula fields are not visible on edit pages.

In account formulas, all business account fields are available as merge fields. However, account fields exclusive to person accounts such as Birthdate and Email are not available.

Reference:

https://help.salesforce.com/s/articleView?id=sf.customize_formulas.htm&type=5

45) A. True

Explanation: A cross-object formula in Salesforce can reference fields from related parent objects, allowing for calculations and logic that involve fields from multiple objects in a single formula.

A cross-object formula can reference merge fields from a master ("parent") object if an object is on the detail side of a master-detail relationship. A cross-object formula also works with lookup relationships.

References:

https://help.salesforce.com/s/articleView?id=sf.customize_cross_object.htm&type=5

https://trailhead.salesforce.com/content/learn/projects/improve-data-quality-for-a-recruiting-app/create-cross-object-formulas

=> These formulas get data from related parent objects to display on the child object.

46) Page layouts are assigned to B. Profiles.

In Salesforce, profiles define a set of permissions and object field visibility settings for users. Page layouts determine how the fields of an object are displayed and arranged on the user interface (UI) for record creation and editing. By assigning page layouts to profiles, administrators can control the way users interact with specific objects based on their roles within the organization.

Page layouts in Salesforce are assigned to profiles, which determine how fields and related lists are displayed to users assigned to those profiles.

Here's why the other options are not correct:

A. Users: While users can inherit page layouts through their assigned profiles, page layouts are not directly assigned to individual users.

C. Roles: Similar to users, roles don't directly receive page layout assignments. Roles are used to group users with similar permission sets, and then profiles are assigned to roles. Profiles ultimately determine the page layouts users can access.

D. Roles & subordinates: This isn't a standard assignment option in Salesforce. Roles manage user groups, and profiles define permissions and page layout access.

Reference:

https://trailhead.salesforce.com/content/learn/modules/lex_customization/lex_customization_page_layouts

=> You can assign page layouts to different user profiles.

After defining page layouts, assign which page layouts users see. A user's profile determines which page layout he or she sees.

47) A. Record Types

Explanation: Record types in Salesforce can be used to filter or segment picklist values based on the user's profile, allowing for different sets of values to be available based on the record type assigned to a particular record.

Reference:

https://help.salesforce.com/s/articleView?id=sf.notes_on_entering_filter_criteria.htm&type=5

=> If your organization uses record types, the lookup dialog lists picklist values for all record types. Use the "equals" or "not equal to" operators for these filters.

48) In Salesforce, business processes are designed to automate and guide users through specific workflows for various objects. Here are the two objects that can utilize business processes:

A. Cases: Business processes can be created for cases to define the stages a case progresses through, from initial submission to resolution. This helps ensure consistent case management and streamlines the process for customer support teams.

B. Opportunities: Sales processes are a type of business process specifically designed for opportunities. They define the stages a potential sale goes through, from initial lead qualification to closing the deal. This provides a roadmap for sales reps and helps track progress within the sales cycle.

Cases and Opportunities in Salesforce can utilize business processes, which are used to standardize and streamline the way work is done in an organization. Business processes define the path that a record follows through its lifecycle, including the stages it goes through and the actions that can be taken at each stage. Campaigns and Knowledge do not typically utilize business processes in the same way as Cases and Opportunities.

Here's why the other options are not applicable:

C. Campaigns: Campaigns are used for marketing initiatives and typically don't have defined stages managed by business processes. However, workflows or automation tools can be used to manage aspects of a campaign.

D. Knowledge: Knowledge articles store information for internal or customer use, and they don't inherently follow a workflow managed by business processes.

"Use multiple business processes to track separate sales, support, and lead lifecycles".

So, Opportunities (Sales), Support (Cases) and leads.

49) Answer: B. Stage

Explanation: The Stage field in a sales process represents the current stage of a sales opportunity, and it is typically modified or filtered as part of defining the sales process.

A sales process in Salesforce defines the various stages an opportunity goes through, from initial lead qualification to closing the deal.

The Stage field on the Opportunity object represents the current position within the sales process.

When a System Administrator creates a sales process, they are essentially defining the available stages (e.g., Prospecting, Qualifying, Negotiation, Closed Won) and the transitions allowed between them.

While other fields like Amount, Close Date, and Next Steps might be relevant to the sales process, they wouldn't be the primary field for modification during sales process creation. Stages are the core elements that structure the entire sales pipeline.

Reference:

https://help.salesforce.com/s/articleView?id=sfdo.SFDO_Create_Opp_Stages_Process.htm&type=5

50) B. A Master - Detail relationship on the Shipment object to the Opportunity object.

Explanation: To establish a close linkage between shipments and opportunities, and to ensure that each shipment is associated with an opportunity, a Master - Detail relationship should be created on the Shipment object to the Opportunity object. This relationship makes the Shipment record dependent on the Opportunity record, ensuring that a Shipment record cannot exist without being associated with an Opportunity.

The clue in the question is the term 'closely linked' which is used to describe M-D relationships.

51) A. True

Explanation: In Salesforce, to create a many-to-many relationship between two objects, you need to create a junction object. This junction object will have Master-Detail relationships with both objects, allowing for a many-to-many relationship to be established and managed.

Reference:

https://help.salesforce.com/s/articleView?id=sf.relationships_manytomany.htm&type=5

52) B. False

Explanation: Adding the related list for Field History Tracking to a page layout is not required to enable Field History Tracking for an object. Field History Tracking can be enabled or disabled for an object in the object's settings, regardless of whether the related list is included in the page layout.

Activating Field History Tracking for an object does not require including the related list in the page layout.

Here's why:

- **Field History Tracking:** This feature records changes made to specific fields within an object over time. It allows you to see who made the change, the date and time, and the previous and new values (depending on settings).

- **Page Layouts:** These define how fields are displayed and arranged on the user interface for record creation and editing. Related lists display information about related records from other objects.

While including the "History" related list in the page layout can provide a convenient way to access field change history directly from the record detail page, it's not mandatory for field history tracking to function.

Here's how you can activate Field History Tracking:

1. Go to the object definition for the desired object.
2. In the object settings, locate the "Fields & Relationships" section.
3. Find the specific field you want to track history for.
4. Click on "Set History Tracking" for that field.

Once enabled for a field, history will be tracked regardless of whether the related list is present in the page layout. Users can access the field history through various methods, including:

- The "History" related list (if included in the page layout)
- The "Audit Trail" link (for users with appropriate permissions)
- Reporting tools (by including the "History" field)

Reference:

When you enable tracking for an object, customize your page layouts to include the object's history related list.

https://help.salesforce.com/s/articleView?id=sf.tracking_field_history_for_custom_objects.htm&type=5

53) B. Salesforce ID

Explanation: To update records using the Data Loader, the CSV file must include the Salesforce ID field for each record. This field uniquely identifies the record and is necessary for the Data Loader to update the correct record.

Data Loader Matching: When updating records, the Data Loader needs a way to uniquely identify the record it should modify. The Salesforce ID provides a permanent and unique identifier for each record in Salesforce, ensuring accurate targeting of the specific record for updates.

Other Fields: While fields like Owner or Record Owner might be included in the CSV for updating ownership during the process, they aren't strictly mandatory for the update operation itself. The Salesforce ID is the key element for record matching and update.

Object Name: While the Data Loader needs to know the object, you're updating (e.g., Opportunity, Contact), this information is typically provided during the Data Loader configuration process and isn't necessarily a specific field within the CSV itself.

Therefore, the Salesforce ID is the crucial field to include in your CSV file for effective record updates using the Salesforce Data Loader.

54) D. All of the above

Explanation: A security token is required to access Salesforce via the Import Wizard, Data Loader, and Salesforce for Outlook. The security token is an additional layer of security used for authentication when accessing Salesforce from outside of the trusted network.

Security tokens are an extra layer of security that Salesforce uses to verify a user's identity when accessing the platform through programmatic methods. This helps prevent unauthorized access, especially when using tools that don't involve the standard Salesforce login flow.

Here's a breakdown of why security tokens are required for these tools:

A. Import Wizard: The Import Wizard is a web-based tool for importing data into Salesforce. While it uses a web interface, it interacts with the Salesforce API behind the scenes. Since it's not a traditional login, a security token is needed for authentication.

B. Data Loader: The Data Loader is a desktop application used for bulk import and export of data in Salesforce. Similar to the Import Wizard, it leverages the Salesforce API and requires a security token for access.

C. Salesforce for Outlook: This integration allows users to manage Salesforce data directly from their Microsoft Outlook environment. Because it interacts with the Salesforce API to perform CRUD (create, read, update, delete) operations on data, a security token is necessary for secure communication.

In conclusion, security tokens are an important safeguard for programmatic access to Salesforce, and they are required for all the tools you mentioned: Import Wizard, Data Loader, and Salesforce for Outlook.

55) B. False. The Data Loader can identify potential duplicate records during the import process, but it cannot handle duplicates automatically.

Here's a breakdown of the Data Loader's behavior regarding duplicates:

Identification: During the import process, the Data Loader can compare incoming data with existing records based on matching criteria you define (usually Salesforce ID or fields like Name and Email). If potential duplicates are found, the Data Loader will flag them for your review.

Manual Handling: The Data Loader relies on you to determine how to handle potential duplicates. You'll need to configure the import process to either:

Skip the duplicate record and continue processing the next record.

Create a new record even if a potential duplicate exists (not recommended as it creates data inconsistencies).

Update an existing record (if the import data contains updated information).

There's no automatic duplicate handling by the Data Loader itself. You need to define the desired behavior through the import configuration.

Import Wizard can do this, be careful not to confuse the two.

56) According to Salesforce documentation and industry best practices, the answer is:

B. False

While the Import Wizard was previously an option for importing Opportunity records in some Salesforce editions, it's generally not recommended or available in current configurations.

Here's why:

Limited Editions: The Import Wizard for Opportunities was primarily available in the Salesforce Essentials edition. For other editions like Professional, Enterprise, and Unlimited, the Data Loader (a separate tool) is the recommended method for importing data, including Opportunities.

Data Loader Capabilities: The Data Loader offers more flexibility and control compared to the Import Wizard. It supports a wider range of objects, allows for scheduling imports, and provides detailed error reports during the import process.

Current Approach:

For importing Opportunity records, the recommended approach is to use the Salesforce Data Loader. It provides a robust and efficient solution for bulk data import into Salesforce.

You can't import these records via the Data Import Wizard:
- Assets
- Cases
- Campaigns
- Contracts
- Documents
- Opportunities
- Products

57) Correct answer: AC

A. The import file should include a record owner for each record: Ensuring that each record in the import file has a specified record owner is crucial to maintaining data integrity and ownership assignments.

C. Data should be de-duplicated in the import file prior to import: De-duplicating data before importing helps prevent the creation of duplicate records, which can cause confusion and data quality issues.

The reason A is important, is that unless an Owner is specified, the Salesforce User doing the import will become the Owner of all the records being imported. That would mean the admin would have to do another data job or use the Mass Transfer tool to change the Owners after the records are created. That will be much harder than setting the Owner before the import.

Reference:

https://trailblazers.salesforce.com/answers?id=90630000000hkilAAA

58) Correct answer: ABD

A. Weekly Data Export

B. Data Loader

D. Reports

Explanation:

A. Weekly Data Export: Salesforce offers a Weekly Data Export feature that allows you to export your organization's data once a week, including all data types and attachments.

B. Data Loader: The Data Loader is a powerful tool provided by Salesforce for importing, exporting, and deleting data in Salesforce, making it suitable for creating backups.

D. Reports: Salesforce reports can be used to extract specific sets of data based on criteria and can be exported to create backups of selected data.

59) A. True

Explanation: In Salesforce, deleted records are stored in the Recycle Bin for up to 15 days before being permanently deleted. During this time, they can be restored if needed.

Deleted records in Salesforce remain in the Recycle Bin for a maximum of 15 days. This provides a window of opportunity for administrators or users with appropriate permissions to restore accidentally deleted records.

Here are some additional details to keep in mind:

The 15-day timer starts from the moment the record is deleted.

Once the 15 days are up, the record is permanently deleted from the Recycle Bin and cannot be recovered through standard methods.

Organizations can configure data backup and recovery solutions to potentially retrieve data even after it's purged from the Recycle Bin, but this usually involves additional tools and services.

It's a good practice to have clear data deletion policies and procedures in place to manage accidental deletions and ensure proper data retention based on your organization's needs.

60) C. Tabular

Explanation: The Tabular report type in Salesforce presents data in a simple list format without any subtotals or groupings.

Here's a breakdown of the report types and their characteristics:

Tabular: This is the most basic report format. It displays rows and columns of data, similar to a spreadsheet, without any automatic grouping or calculations. It's ideal for getting a quick overview of your data.

Summary: Summary reports allow you to group rows of data and see subtotals or other calculations for each group. They provide a higher level of data analysis compared to tabular reports.

Matrix: Matrix reports are more complex and display data in a grid format with both row and column groupings. They can include subtotals and calculations for various levels of grouping.

Custom: Custom reports are those you create yourself, and they can leverage any of the formatting options (tabular, summary, matrix) depending on your design.

Standard: Standard reports are pre-built reports provided by Salesforce for common objects and use cases. They can be tabular, summary, or matrix reports depending on the specific standard report.

Therefore, for a basic list of data without subtotals, the tabular report format is the most suitable choice in Salesforce.

Reference:

https://winsurtech.com/blog/salesforce-reports/

PRACTICE TEST II

1) Use Custom Summary Formulas to create calculated summaries on numerical fields in _____ and _____ reports.

A. Tabular and Summary

B. Custom and Standard

C. Summary and Matrix

D. Matrix and Tabular

2) Which of the following statements accurately describes custom summary formulas?

A. Reports can be grouped by a custom summary formula result.

B. Custom summary formulas can reference a formula field within a report.

C. Custom summary formulas can reference another custom summary formula.

D. Custom summary formulas can be used in a report built from a custom report type.

3) The following statements are true regarding scheduling and emailing reports.

A. The running user determines whose data is visible on the report.

B. The running user must have access to the folder in which the report is saved.

C. All email recipients must have access to the same folder.

D. The report is emailed within 30 minutes of the Preferred Start Time.

E. All of the above.

4) A Dashboard is a visual representation of data from multiple reports and (Select four answer choices).

A. Is comprised of up to 20 components.

B. Displays data from standard reports.

C. Has a running user to determine what data is visible.

D. Displays data as of the last time the dashboard was refreshed.

E. Always shows up to date data.

F. Can be scheduled to be refreshed and emailed automatically.

5) Users can share a snapshot of a component on a dashboard to the dashboard feed, a user feed, or a group feed. This feature is known as:

A. Dashboard Component Snapshot.

B. The Running User.

C. Chatter Groups.

D. Dashboard Component.

E. Dynamic Dashboards.

6) Dynamic Dashboards enable data to be presented based on the user viewing it, rather than being tied to a specified running user, thus eliminating the necessity to create multiple versions of the same dashboard for different users.

A. True

B. False

7) What feature enables a Sales VP to view dashboard data by region within their territory?

A. Dynamic Dashboards.

B. Dashboard Filters.

C. Dashboard Snapshots.

D. This is not possible.

8) The System Administrator has been tasked with ensuring that an email is sent to Sales Ops when an opportunity is closed, notifying them of the closed deal. What evaluation criteria will the system admin use for the workflow rule?

A. When a record is created.

B. When a record is created or updated.

C. When a record is created/updated and didn't previously meet the trigger criteria.

D. None of the above.

9) The support team has requested the System Administrator to automate the notification of a customer's support plan ending. They want the Customer Support Rep to receive an email 30 days before the Support Plan Expires, which is recorded on the Account record. What will the system administrator do?

A. Create a workflow rule with a time-based trigger to fire 30 days before the Support Plan Expiration Date and use an email action to notify the assigned Support Rep.

B. Create a workflow rule with an immediate action to email the Support rep but with a due date of 30 days before the Support Expiration Date.

C. Create an Apex trigger to fire 30 days before Support Plan Expiration Date and use an email action to notify the assigned Support Rep.

D. This cannot be done.

10) The system administrator was testing workflow rules and needs to remove pending time-based workflow actions. How can they accomplish this?

A. Delete the workflow rule.

B. Deactivate the workflow rule.

C. Delete the actions in the Time-based Workflow queue.

D. Reset passwords for all users of the org.

E. None of the above.

11) What feature would a system administrator enable to allow prospects/customers of AW Computing to fill out a form on the corporate website and have that information automatically converted into a lead in Salesforce?

A. Auto Response Rules

B. Assignment Rules

C. Web-to-Lead

D. Escalation Rules

12) When a Lead is converted, an Account, Contact and _____ record are created.

A. Lead

B. Case

C. Campaign

D. Opportunity

13) Queues can consist of the following: (choose three answers)

A. Users

B. Public Groups

C. Roles

D. Profiles

E. External Chatter Users

14) Assignment rules automatically assign Leads and Cases to users and queues based on criteria set by the system administrator.

A. True

B. False

15) The system administrator needs to ensure that all Leads originating from the website are assigned to a website lead queue, that Leads from a recent trade show are assigned to Matt Wilson, and that all other leads are assigned to Phil Smith. The system administrator will:

A. Create 3 assignment rules.

B. Create 1 assignment rule with multiple criteria entries.

C. Create an assignment rule and 2 workflow rules.

D. Use workflow rules to accomplish this.

16) Auto response rules can be utilized to send personalized, automated responses to customers based on the details they provide through the Web-to-Lead form.

A. True

B. False

17) When Chatter is activated in an organization, the following occurs. (choose three answers)

A. The Chatter app is added to the Force.com app menu.

B. The Chatter tab is added to all standard apps.

C. Accounts, Contacts, Cases, Leads and Opportunities are enabled for Chatter.

D. All users are added to the All-Chatter group.

E. All of the above.

18) With a Chatter Free license, users can access People, Profiles, Groups, and Files, in addition to: (choose four answers)

A. Make posts

B. View comments

C. Upload files

D. Join groups

E. View records

19) Chatter External licenses permit users external to the company to participate in public Chatter groups.

A. True

B. False

20) Who has the ability to invite Chatter customers to join a Chatter group? (choose two answers)

A. The system admin.

B. Group owner.

C. All Chatter users.

D. None of the above.

21) Folders are utilized to organize the following (Select all that apply.)

A. Dashboards

B. Reports

C. Documents

D. Email templates

E. All of the above

F. None of the above

22) The _____ determines if a user can read, create and edit Contact records, the _____ determines if he can see/edit contact records owned by his subordinates.

A. Role, Profile

B. OWD, Sharing rules

C. Sharing rules, Role Hierarchy

D. Profile, Role

23) If the page layout displays the Next Steps field on an Opportunity record, but the Field Level Security settings hide the field, how will the field appear to the user?

A. The field will be hidden from the user.

B. The field will be read only.

C. The field will be visible and editable to the user.

D. None of the above.

24) Record types define the following components.

A. Picklist values

B. Page layouts

C. Business processes

D. All of the above

E. None of the above

25) Which objects are compatible with business processes? (choose four answers)

A. Opportunities

B. Leads

C. Campaigns

D. Accounts

E. Solutions

F. Cases

G. Contacts

26) Lead assignment rules automatically assign leads to

owners and queues based on criteria defined by the system administrator within the rule.

A. True

B. False

27) Which of the following actions are initiated by workflow rules? (choose four answers)

A. Email

B. Task

C. Field update

D. Record update

E. Record creation

F. Outbound message

G. Time trigger

28) Do two different users receive identical search results when searching for a common keyword?

A. Yes

B. No

29) What occurs if a lead is converted without a value in the company field?

A. A Business Account is created.

B. A Person Account is created.

C. You will be prompted to decide whether to create a Person or a Business Account.

D. Nothing.

30) An Approval Process starts when a record is:

A. Created

B. Saved

C. Edited

D. Submitted for Approval

31) A time-based workflow can be triggered whenever a record is created or updated.

A. True

B. False

32) When you add a custom object tab, all of the following will be accessible with the object EXCEPT which one?

A. Recent Items.

B. Sidebar Search.

C. Added to New Link/Create New Object Drop Down.

D. Custom Object Reports.

33) When you delete a lead from a campaign, it also deletes the

lead record.

A. True

B. False

34) Which Salesforce application helps organizations accelerate and simplify every stage of the sales process?

A. SF ideas

B. SF content

C. SF Automation

D. SF Customer service and support

35) All of the following objects can have a queue, EXCEPT which one?

A. Accounts

B. Cases

C. Leads

D. Custom Objects

36) You can utilize standard reports in the creation of Dashboards.

A. True

B. False

37) Who has the ability to select the "sharing" button on Account and Opportunity records?

A. The Record Owner, System Administrator, and a User shared to the record.

B. The Record Owner, a User shared to the record, and any User above the Record Owner in the Role Hierarchy.

C. The Record Owner, a User above the Record Owner, and the System Administrator.

D. The Record Owner and System Administrator.

38) You're assisting a Professional Edition organization that wants to install the Expense Tracker application, which necessitates the utilization of 4 custom tabs, 3 custom objects, and one custom app. If the company is already using 4 applications, 36 custom objects, and 7 custom tabs, what will happen when they try to install Expense
Tracker?

A. They will not be able to complete the installation process as they have reached the maximum number of custom tabs.

B. They will not be able to complete the installation process as they have reached the maximum number of custom objects.

C. The installation will succeed.

D. The installation will succeed, but only the reports.

39) Your organization is a US-based company with the default currency set to US Dollars. As a sales rep, your personal currency is set to British Pounds. You create an opportunity with the

currency in British Pounds. The administrator then updates the currency conversion rates. Which of the following best describes what happens to the amount of your British-Pound-based opportunity?

A. The overall opportunity amount does not change but the converted amount in a report does.

B. The overall opportunity amount and converted amount in a report change.

C. Only newly created opportunities reflect the change.

D. Only historically created opportunities reflect the change.

40) Custom Links can be utilized for the following purposes:

A. Launching an External URL

B. Running an S Control

C. Running a report

D. All of the Above

41) It is possible to manually share a record of a custom object.

A. True

B. False

42) You can customize the related list for Opportunity Stage History on an Opportunity Page Layout.

A. True

B. False

43) Which of the following is not a way to view a forecast?

A. Territory

B. Product Family

C. Date Range

D. Sales Team

44) What is controlled by a Profile?

A. Username and Password.

B. Role level access.

C. Read, Create, Edit, and Delete permissions.

D. Sharing rules.

45) When a lead with a single marketing campaign is converted, the campaign information will automatically map to the newly created contact and opportunity records.

A. True

B. False

46) Related Lists display records from the "many" sides of a one-to-many relationship.

A. True

B. False

47) Case Assignment Rules are triggered based on the time elapsed since the case was created.

A. True
B. False

48) Which statements accurately describe the Master/Detail relationship in custom objects? (choose two answers)

A. Sharing is inherited from parent.
B. Child needs to be manually deleted when parent is deleted.
C. Only child fields are available for reporting.
D. Lookup field child is required.

49) When test driving an application on the AppExchange Directory, you cannot view the S-Control configurations of that application.

A. True
B. False

50) Validation rules can assess an opportunity line item against the opportunity with which it is linked.

A. True

B. false

51) If a profile lacks access to an application, it will also lack access to the tabs and objects associated with that application.

A. True

B. False

52) Which type of field is unable to be universally required?

A. Lookup

B. Text

C. Email

D. Number

53) Custom Web Tab can include all of the following EXCEPT:

A. A URL.

B. A URL that passes salesforce.com data like an organization's name.

C. An S-Control.

D. An S-Control snippet.

54) To which sets of objects in Salesforce.com can custom lead fields be mapped?

A. Account, Contact, Opportunity, or Campaigns.

B. Account, Contact, or Opportunity.

C. Account or Contact Only.

D. Contact or Opportunity Only.

55) Which of the following objects can you map a custom lead field to at a single instance? (Choose three answers)

A. Account

B. Contacts

C. Cases

D. Opportunities

56) Even after a field has been hidden from a Profile using 'Field Level Security', a User associated with that Profile can still view the field using which of the following methods:

A. List Views

B. Reports

C. Search

D. None of the above, the user cannot see the field at all

57) Can a person account be related to a contact on a business account?

A. True

B. False

58) How is the expected revenue determined in an opportunity?

A. Amount multiplied by the total price of all opportunity line items.

B. The sales price on any line-item times the probability of the opportunity.

C. Opportunity Amount multiplied by the probability.

D. Amount multiplied by the discount percent.

59) Which of the following objects can a custom lookup field be added to in order to establish a relationship with a standard object?

A. Users and Custom Objects.

B. Leads, Accounts, Contacts and Custom Objects.

C. Users, Custom Objects and Campaigns.

D. Custom Objects, Contract and Campaigns.

60) If the Organization Wide Default sharing is set to private for all objects and no sharing rules have been created, can two users in the Sales Rep Role view each other's data?

A. Yes

B. No

ANSWERS AND EXPLANATIONS

1) The correct answer is C. Summary and Matrix.

Custom Summary Formulas can be used to create calculated summaries on numerical fields in Summary and Matrix reports in Salesforce. Summary reports display grouped data, and Matrix reports display data in a grid format with both row and column groupings. Custom Summary Formulas allow you to perform calculations on the grouped data and display the results in the report.

2) The correct answer is B. Custom summary formulas can reference a formula field within a report.

Explanation:

A. Reports can be grouped by a custom summary formula result - Incorrect. Custom summary formulas are used to calculate summary values, but they do not directly control grouping in reports.

B. Custom summary formulas can reference a formula field within a report - Correct. Custom summary formulas can reference other fields, including formula fields, to calculate summary values.

C. Custom summary formulas can reference another custom summary formula - Incorrect. Custom summary formulas cannot directly reference other custom summary formulas.

D. Custom summary formulas can be used in a report built from a custom report type - Correct. Custom summary formulas can be used in reports based on custom report types, as long as the fields they reference are available in the report type.

3) The correct answer is E. All of the above.

Explanation:

A. The running user determines whose data is visible on the report - True. The data visible on the report is determined by the permissions and access level of the running user.

B. The running user must have access to the folder in which the report is saved - True. The running user needs access to the folder to run the report and schedule it for emailing.

C. All email recipients must have access to the same folder - True. Email recipients need access to the folder to view the report attached to the email.

D. The report is emailed within 30 minutes of the Preferred Start Time - True. Salesforce aims to send the report within 30 minutes of the preferred start time, but actual delivery time may vary.

Points to consider when Scheduling Reports:

1. You can't create schedules for joined reports.

2. Your organization is limited to no more than 200 scheduled reports. Additional scheduled reports may be available for purchase.

3. Scheduled reports run in the time zone of the user who set up the schedule.

4. The report runs within 30 minutes of the time you select for Preferred Start Time.

5. Scheduling reports is not tracked in the audit trail history.

6. The access level of the running user determines what other users, including portal users, see when they receive the scheduled report run results.

7. You can send reports only to email addresses included on Salesforce user records.

4) Correct answer: ACDF

A. Is comprised of up to 20 components.

C. Has a running user to determine what data is visible.

D. Displays data as of the last time the dashboard was refreshed.

F. Can be scheduled to be refreshed and emailed automatically.

Explanation:

A. Is comprised of up to 20 components - True. A dashboard can have up to 20 components, which can include charts, tables, metrics, and other visual representations of data.

B. Displays data from standard reports - Not necessarily. While dashboards can display data from reports, they can also show data from other sources.

C. Has a running user to determine what data is visible - True. The running user's permissions determine which data is visible on the dashboard.

D. Displays data as of the last time the dashboard was refreshed - True. The data on a dashboard is based on the last refresh of the dashboard.

E. Always shows up-to-date data - Not necessarily. The data on a dashboard is only as current as the last refresh.

F. Can be scheduled to be refreshed and emailed automatically - True. Dashboards can be scheduled to refresh and email automatically to specified recipients.

5) The correct answer is A. Dashboard Component Snapshot.

Explanation:

A. Dashboard Component Snapshot - Correct. This feature allows users to share a snapshot of a component on a dashboard to the dashboard feed, a user feed, or a group feed.

B. The Running User - Incorrect. The running user refers to the user whose permissions determine the data visible on the dashboard.

C. Chatter Groups - Incorrect. Chatter groups are a collaboration feature in Salesforce and are not directly related to sharing dashboard snapshots.

D. Dashboard Component - Incorrect. While this answer is close, it does not specify the action of sharing a snapshot of a component.

E. Dynamic Dashboards - Incorrect. Dynamic dashboards allow users to view different data based on their permissions, but they are not directly related to sharing snapshots of dashboard components.

6) A. True

Explanation: Dynamic Dashboards in Salesforce allow data to be displayed based on the user viewing the dashboard, rather than being tied to a specific running user. This functionality eliminates the need to create multiple versions of the same dashboard for different users, as the dashboard dynamically adjusts its data based on the user's permissions and settings.

Dynamic dashboards are designed to address the very issue mentioned in the statement.

Here's why:

Traditional dashboards display the same data for all users, regardless of their role or needs. This can lead to information overload for some users and lack of relevant information for others.

Dynamic dashboards overcome this limitation by tailoring the displayed data based on the user viewing it. This is achieved through features like:

User filters: Users can see data specific to their department, region, or other relevant criteria.

Row-level security: Restricts data visibility based on user permissions.

Conditional formatting: Highlights specific data points based on user roles.

By dynamically adjusting the content, dynamic dashboards eliminate the need to create numerous versions of the same dashboard for different user groups.

7) B. Dashboard Filters.

Explanation: Dashboard filters allow users to narrow down the data displayed on a dashboard based on specific criteria, such as region. By applying a region filter, the Sales VP can view dashboard data specific to each region within their territory.

Dynamic Dashboards are a broader concept that allows for user-specific data display based on various factors, but they don't guarantee regional filtering specifically.

Dashboard Filters empower users to interact with the dashboard and filter the data based on their needs. In this case, the Sales VP can leverage a regional filter to view data by specific regions within their territory.

Dashboard Snapshots capture a static image of the dashboard at a particular point, and wouldn't enable dynamic filtering by region.

This is not possible is incorrect. Salesforce dashboards with filters provide the functionality for regional viewing.

Reference:

htttps://help.salesforce.com/s/articleView?id=sf.dashboard_filters_overview.htm&type=5

8) The correct answer is:

B. When a record is created or updated.

Here's why:

When a record is created. - This wouldn't capture existing opportunities that get closed later.

When a record is created/updated and didn't previously meet the trigger criteria. - This is a bit more complex than necessary. We simply need the rule to fire whenever an opportunity is closed, regardless of its previous state.

B. When a record is created or updated - This is the most suitable option. It ensures the workflow rule triggers whenever an opportunity record is created (new opportunity) or updated (existing opportunity being closed).

By selecting this criteria, the workflow rule will activate whenever an opportunity is closed, allowing the system administrator to include sending an email notification to Sales Ops within the workflow actions.

9) The correct answer is:

A. Create a workflow rule with a time-based trigger to fire 30 days before the Support Plan Expiration Date and use an email action to notify the assigned Support Rep.

Here's why the other options are not ideal:

B. Create a workflow rule with an immediate action to email the Support rep but with a due date of 30 days before the Support Expiration Date. - Workflow rules with immediate actions typically execute right away, not on a scheduled basis.

C. Create an Apex trigger to fire 30 days before Support Plan Expiration Date and use an email action to notify the assigned Support Rep. - While Apex triggers can achieve this functionality, workflow rules are a simpler and more declarative approach for this scenario.

D. This cannot be done. - This is incorrect. Salesforce workflows offer time-based triggers and email actions, making this automation achievable.

By creating a workflow rule with a time-based trigger set for 30 days before the "Support Plan Expiration Date" field on the Account record, the system administrator can ensure an email notification gets sent to the assigned Support Rep automatically.

10) The correct answer is:

C. Delete the actions in the Time-based Workflow queue.

Here's why the other options are not suitable:

A. Delete the workflow rule. - While this would eventually remove the pending actions, it's an unnecessarily drastic step. Deleting the rule would require recreating it later.

B. Deactivate the workflow rule. - Deactivating the rule prevents future actions from being created, but it doesn't remove existing pending actions in the queue.

D. Reset passwords for all users of the org. - This is completely unrelated to workflow actions and would be a very disruptive solution.

E. None of the above. - Eliminating all other options leaves C as the viable answer.

By accessing the Time-based Workflow queue (found in Setup > Monitoring > Time-Based Workflow), the system administrator can identify pending actions associated with the workflow rule being tested. Selecting and deleting those specific actions will remove them from the queue without affecting the workflow rule itself.

11) The correct answer is:

C. Web-to-Lead

Here's why:

Auto Response Rules automate email responses based on specific criteria but wouldn't handle lead capture from a website form.

Assignment Rules define how leads are automatically assigned to sales reps, not how they are created.

Web-to-Lead is a specifically designed Salesforce feature that allows website forms to automatically generate leads in Salesforce. When a prospect submits a form, their information is mapped to corresponding lead fields, creating a new lead record.

Escalation Rules define how cases are escalated based on specific criteria, not relevant to lead capture.

12) The correct answer is: D. Opportunity

When a lead is converted in Salesforce, it typically triggers the creation of three records:

Account: This record represents the company or organization associated with the lead.

Contact: This record represents the individual within the company (lead) you're trying to establish a business relationship with.

Opportunity: This record represents a potential sales deal or opportunity associated with the converted lead. It's not mandatory to create an opportunity during lead conversion, but it's a common practice to track potential sales.

13) Correct answer: ABC

A. Users

B. Public Groups

C. Roles

Explanation: Queues in Salesforce can consist of individual Users, Public Groups, and Roles. These entities can be assigned to a queue to manage and distribute work efficiently among team members or roles. External Chatter Users and Profiles are not typically included in queues.

14) A. True

Explanation: Assignment rules in Salesforce are used to automatically assign Leads and Cases to users and queues based on criteria defined by the system administrator. This helps streamline the process of assigning and managing incoming Leads and Cases.

Assignment rules are a valuable automation tool within Salesforce for streamlining lead and case distribution. Here's how they work:

System administrators define criteria based on various fields within Leads or Cases (e.g., industry, product interest, location).

Multiple criteria entries can be established within a single assignment rule to handle different scenarios.

When a new Lead or Case is created that meets the specified criteria in an assignment rule, it gets automatically assigned to a designated user or queue.

This automation helps ensure leads and cases are routed to the most appropriate resources based on predefined conditions, improving lead nurturing and case resolution efficiency.

15) B. Create 1 assignment rule with multiple criteria entries.

Explanation: To achieve the required assignment logic, the system administrator can create a single assignment rule with multiple criteria entries. Each criteria entry can specify a different condition for assigning Leads to the appropriate queue or user.

This approach is more efficient than creating separate assignment rules or using workflow rules for this purpose.

A. Create 3 assignment rules. - This would work, but it's less efficient. One assignment rule with multiple criteria entries can handle all three situations.

C. Create an assignment rule and 2 workflow rules. - Workflow rules are not ideal for lead assignment based on origin. Assignment rules are specifically designed for this purpose.

D. Use workflow rules to accomplish this. - Similar to option C, workflow rules are not the most suitable tool for lead assignment based on origin. Assignment rules are a more streamlined approach.

By creating a single assignment rule with multiple criteria entries, the system administrator can define specific conditions for each scenario:

Criteria Entry 1: Lead Source equals "Website" - Assign to Website Lead Queue.

Criteria Entry 2: Lead Source equals "Trade Show" - Assign to Matt Wilson.

Else: Assign to Phil Smith (as a catch-all for any remaining leads not matching the first two criteria).

This approach ensures efficient lead routing based on their origin, reducing manual intervention and ensuring leads reach the appropriate teams or individuals.

16) A. True

Explanation: Auto response rules in Salesforce can indeed be used to send personalized, automated responses to customers based on the information they provide through the Web-to-Lead form. This helps in acknowledging the customer's inquiry or submission and provides them with relevant information or next steps.

17) Correct answer: ABC

A. The Chatter app is added to the Force.com app menu.

B. The Chatter tab is added to all standard apps.

C. Accounts, Contacts, Cases, Leads, and Opportunities are enabled for Chatter.

Explanation: When Chatter is activated in an organization, the Chatter app is added to the Force.com app menu, the Chatter tab is added to all standard apps, and standard objects such as Accounts, Contacts, Cases, Leads, and Opportunities are enabled for Chatter collaboration. Users are not automatically added to the All-Chatter group.

18) Correct answer: ABCD

A. Make posts

B. View comments

C. Upload files

D. Join groups

Explanation: With a Chatter Free license, users can access People, Profiles, Groups, and Files, as well as make posts, view comments, upload files, and join groups. However, they cannot view records unless they have access to the corresponding Salesforce objects through other means (e.g., through a Salesforce platform license).

A. Make posts - Yes, Chatter Free users can create posts to share information and updates with others.

B. View comments - Yes, they can see comments posted by others on feeds, profiles, and groups they have access to.

C. Upload files - Yes, Chatter Free users can upload files (with limitations of 5MB per file and 25MB total storage) to share with others.

D. Join groups - Yes, they can join existing public Chatter groups to participate in discussions and collaboration.

E. View records - No, users with a Chatter Free license cannot directly view details of Salesforce records (like Accounts, Contacts, Opportunities) through Chatter. They can only see basic information about the record through mentions or feeds, but clicking on it wouldn't grant them full access to the record details.

So, Chatter Free users have some capabilities for social collaboration within Salesforce, but their access is restricted compared to users with full Salesforce licenses.

19) B. False

Explanation: Chatter External licenses do not allow users outside the company to join public Chatter groups. These licenses are intended for users external to the organization to access specific Salesforce objects and data shared with them, but they do not provide access to Chatter groups.

Chatter External

This license is for users who are outside of your company's

email domain. These external users, also called customers, can be invited to Chatter groups that allow customers. Customers can access information and interact with users only in the groups they're invited to. They have no access to Chatter objects or data. Chatter External users can view user profiles, but they can't edit them.

Even if you have Chatter External, you need to create a private group to add customers.

Reference:

If customer invitations are enabled for your organization, you can invite, add, and remove customers. It must be a private group that you own or manage and that allows customers.

https://help.salesforce.com/s/articleView?id=sf.collab_external_adding.htm&type=5

20) Here's who can invite Chatter customers to join a Chatter group:

A. The system admin - The system administrator can also invite Chatter customers to groups, but they likely wouldn't manage individual group invitations directly. Their role is more focused on enabling the "Allow Customers" feature for specific groups and managing Chatter External licenses.

B. Group owner - The owner of a public Chatter group with "Allow Customers" enabled has the ability to invite Chatter customers (users with Chatter External licenses) to join the group.

Both the system admin and the group owner have the ability to invite Chatter customers to join a Chatter group. All Chatter users do not have this ability by default; it is limited to the admin and group owners.

Here's why the other options are not applicable:

C. All Chatter users - Not all Chatter users have the ability to invite external users. This permission is typically limited to group owners or admins with the appropriate settings.

D. None of the above - Eliminating all other options leaves B and A as the most likely ones with the invitation capability.

21) The correct answer is: E. All of the above

Folders are a valuable tool for organizing various elements within Salesforce:

A. Dashboards: Folders help categorize dashboards for easier navigation and access. You can group dashboards by department, function, or any other relevant criteria.

B. Reports: Similar to dashboards, folders can be used to organize reports based on topic, department, or any other logical grouping.

C. Documents: Salesforce offers libraries for document storage, and within these libraries, folders can be created to further organize documents related to specific projects, clients, or stages in the sales process.

D. Email templates: While not a standard Salesforce feature, some third-party applications or custom configurations might allow you to store and manage email templates within folders for better organization.

Reference:

A folder is a place where you can store reports, dashboards, documents, or email templates. Folders can be public, hidden, or shared, and can be set to read-only or read/write. You control who has access to its contents based on roles, permissions, public groups, and license types. You can make a folder available to your entire organization, or make it private so that only the owner has access.

https://help.salesforce.com/s/articleView?id=sf.customize_folders.htm&type=5

22) D. Profile, Role is the most accurate answer in this specific scenario.

Here's why:

The question directly asks about a user's ability to read, create, and edit Contact records. Profiles define these fundamental permissions for objects like Contacts.

Role Hierarchy is not directly relevant to a user's ability to perform CRUD (Create, Read, Update, Delete) operations on their own contacts. It comes into play when considering visibility of contacts owned by subordinates, which wasn't the specific focus of the question.

While Sharing Rules can further refine access beyond the profile permissions, the question emphasizes the initial definition of permissions, which falls under profiles.

Therefore, in this case, option D. Profile, Role is the most precise answer because it addresses the core aspects of user permissions for creating, reading, and editing contact records through profiles and the potential influence of roles on visibility within the hierarchy structure.

23) The correct answer is: A. The field will be hidden from the

user.

Here's why:

Field Level Security takes precedence over page layouts in Salesforce. This means that even if the "Next Steps" field is included on the page layout, if the field-level security settings are set to hide the field for the user, it won't be visible.

Here's a breakdown of the other options:

B. The field will be read only. - While field-level security can restrict editing, it can also completely hide the field. In this case, hiding is the intended outcome.

C. The field will be visible and editable to the user. - This would only happen if the field-level security allows the user to see and edit the field, which isn't the case here.

D. None of the above. - Eliminating all other options leaves A as the most likely scenario.

Remember, field-level security offers granular control over data visibility and editability, overriding the layout configuration when there's a conflict.

24) D. All of the above

Explanation: Record types in Salesforce can define picklist values, page layouts, and business processes. They allow for customization of these components based on the specific requirements of different record types.

Record types are a powerful feature in Salesforce that allows you to customize how different sets of records within the same object are managed. They can define various aspects of the record, including:

A. Picklist values: Record types can control which picklist values are available for specific fields. For example, an Opportunity record type for "New Business" might have different sales stage picklist options compared to an Opportunity record type for "Renewal."

B. Page layouts: Different record types can utilize unique page layouts, ensuring the user interface reflects the specific information relevant to that record type. For instance, a "Donation" Opportunity record type might have a different layout compared to a "Product Sales" Opportunity record type.

C. Business processes: While not as common, record types can be associated with specific business processes, guiding users through the appropriate steps for that particular record type.

So, record types offer a comprehensive approach to customizing record management within Salesforce.

25) Correct answer: ABEF

A. Opportunities

B. Leads

E. Solutions

F. Cases

Here's a breakdown of each term:

Opportunities: These represent potential sales deals that are currently being pursued by the sales team.

Leads: These are potential customers who have shown some interest in a product or service, but haven't yet progressed to the sales stage.

Solutions: These are the products or services offered by a company that address the needs or problems of their customers.

Cases: These refer to situations where a customer requires support or has an issue that needs to be resolved.

Use multiple business processes to display different picklist values according to each user's profile.

- Sales Processes- Opportunities
- Lead Processes- Leads
- Support Processes- Cases
- Solution Processes- Solution

26) B. False

Explanation: Lead assignment rules in Salesforce can indeed automatically assign leads to owners and queues based on criteria specified by the system administrator.

While lead assignment rules are intended to automate lead distribution, they don't directly assign leads to owners. Instead, they establish a set of criteria to determine the most suitable owner or queue for a lead. The system administrator sets these criteria, and the system assigns the lead based on the matching criteria.

Not Owners, but Users and Queue.

Lead Assignment Rules ->Rule Entries->Step 3: Select the user or queue to assign the Lead to.

27) Correct answer: ABCF

A. Email: Workflows can trigger automated emails to be sent to specific recipients based on defined criteria.

B. Task: Tasks can be assigned to users or groups to take action on a record when a workflow rule is triggered.

C. Field update: Specific fields within a record can be automatically updated based on the conditions set in the workflow rule.

F. Outbound message: Workflows can be configured to send secure messages in a specific format (often XML) to external systems.

Not initiated by workflow rules:

D. Record update: This is a broader term encompassing any changes made to a record, which could be manual edits or the result of a workflow rule. Workflows initiate specific field updates, not general record updates.

E. Record creation: While workflows can be triggered by record creation, they don't directly create new records themselves.

G. Time trigger: This refers to a specific type of workflow rule execution based on a scheduled time, not an action itself.

When a record meets all the criteria for a workflow rule, that rule's actions are executed. Workflow rules can help automate the following types of actions based on your organization's processes:

Tasks: Assign a new task to a user, role, or record owner.

Email Alerts: Send an email to one or more recipients you specify.

Field Updates: Update the value of a field on a record.

Outbound Messages: Send a secure, configurable API message (in XML format) to a designated listener.

28) B. No

Explanation: Two different users may receive different search results when searching for a common keyword, as the search results can be influenced by various factors such as the user's permissions, the sharing settings, and the content they have access to.

Here's why two users might not receive identical search results:

Search personalization: Search engines like Google often personalize results based on factors like user location, search history, and past interactions. This means users in different locations or with different search habits might see different results for the same keyword.

Device and browser: The device and browser used can also influence results to a minor extent. For example, a search on a mobile device might prioritize mobile-friendly websites.

Real-time updates: Search results are constantly being updated based on new information and user activity. So, there's a chance that results might differ slightly between users searching at the same time.

However, search engines strive to deliver the most relevant results for each user's query. While there might be some variation, the core results for a common keyword will likely be quite similar for different users.

Not all users have the same access rights. So, User A will see what is available/accessible to them compare to User B.

29) B. A Person Account is created.

Explanation: If a lead is converted without a value in the company field, Salesforce will create a Person Account.

In Salesforce, when you convert a lead, the system typically creates a new record (often an account and a contact) based on the lead information.

The "company field" is a crucial piece of data that helps identify whether the lead represents a business or an individual.

If the company field is left blank during conversion, Salesforce relies on the person accounts feature (if enabled) to handle the situation.

Person Accounts Explained:

Person accounts are a specific type of account record designed to represent individual customers or freelancers.

They are particularly useful when the lead doesn't represent a traditional company but rather a single person.

What Happens When Person Accounts Are Disabled?

If your Salesforce organization doesn't have person accounts enabled, attempting to convert a lead without a company name will likely result in an error.

The system requires a company name for standard business accounts, and without person accounts available, it has nowhere to store the lead data.

Additional Considerations:

Some Salesforce configurations might allow customization of lead conversion behavior for blank company fields, even with person accounts disabled. This could involve creating a placeholder company record or prompting the user to enter a company name.

It's always good practice to ensure the company field is filled whenever possible for better data organization and more efficient sales and marketing activities.

Leads that don't have a value in the Company field are converted to person accounts.

Leads that do have a value in the Company field are converted to business accounts.

30) D. Submitted for Approval

Explanation: The Approval Process is triggered when a record is submitted for approval, not when it is created, saved, or edited.

Approval processes in Salesforce are designed to automate the process of reviewing and approving specific records before they are finalized.

These records typically go through a defined sequence of steps, involving designated approvers who make decisions.

Stages of an Approval Process:

Initiation: The process triggers based on predefined criteria. In this case, the key criterion is that the record is submitted for approval. This submission act initiates the workflow.

Routing: The system routes the record to the first approver according to the established rules within the approval process.

Review and Action: Each approver reviews the record and decides to approve, reject, or request changes.

Iterations (optional): If changes are requested, the record might be sent back to the submitter for modifications and resubmission.

Finalization: Once all approvals are complete, the record receives its final status (approved, rejected, etc.).

Other Record Actions Don't Trigger Approval Processes:

A. Created or B. Saved: Simply creating or saving a record doesn't automatically trigger an approval process. Data entry might be followed by submission for approval, but that's a separate step.

C. Edited: Editing a record might trigger an approval process only if the edits meet specific criteria defined in the process settings. Just any edit wouldn't necessarily lead to approval steps.

By understanding when an approval process starts, you can effectively utilize this automation feature in Salesforce to manage approvals for critical records.

31) B. False

While time-based workflows can be triggered by updates to records, they aren't directly triggered just by creation or any update. They are triggered based on a specific time criteria defined in the workflow.

32) Answer: D. Custom Object Reports.

Explanation: When you add a custom object tab in Salesforce, you can access the custom object through recent items, sidebar search, and it is added to the new link/create new object drop-down. However, custom object reports are not automatically accessible; you need to create reports for the custom object separately.

33) B. False

Deleting a lead from a campaign does not delete the lead record itself. It only removes the lead from the specific campaign it was associated with. The lead record will still exist in your system, but it won't be part of that campaign anymore.

A Lead is related to a Campaign via an object called Campaign Member. When "deleting" a Lead from a Campaign, you are effectively deleting the Campaign Member record, not the Lead record itself.

34) Answer: C. SF Automation

Explanation: Salesforce Automation (SF Automation) helps organizations streamline their sales processes by automating repetitive tasks, managing leads and opportunities, and providing insights to drive sales effectiveness.

Here's why the other options are less likely:

A. SF Ideas: While SF Ideas can be used to capture sales ideas and feedback, it's not directly focused on automating the sales process itself.

B. SF Content: SF Content focuses on managing and sharing content, which can be helpful for sales enablement, but it doesn't directly automate sales workflows.

D. SF Customer Service and Support: This application is geared towards managing customer interactions after a sale, not the sales process itself.

Salesforce Automation, often referred to as Sales Cloud, offers a suite of tools designed to automate repetitive tasks, manage leads and opportunities, and track sales performance. This helps streamline the sales process and improve efficiency.

Reference:

https://help.salesforce.com/articleView?id=extend_click_process.htm&type=5

35) A. Accounts cannot have a queue in Salesforce.

Salesforce queues are designed for objects that represent work items that need to be distributed and assigned to team members. Accounts typically represent static data about your customers and don't need to be routed or assigned for work purposes.

Here's a breakdown of the other options that can have queues:

B. Cases: Queues are commonly used for managing and distributing cases (customer support issues) among support agents.

C. Leads: Queues can be helpful for routing and assigning leads (potential customers) to sales reps.

D. Custom Objects: You can create queues for custom objects that represent work items specific to your organization's needs.

We can use Queues for managing cases, leads, tasks, contact requests, orders, service contracts, knowledge articles, and custom objects.

36) A. True

You can definitely utilize standard reports in the creation of Dashboards in Salesforce. In fact, it's a common and efficient way to leverage existing data analysis for a more visual representation on dashboards. Standard reports provide pre-built structures for specific objects and data points, allowing you to easily include them in your dashboards.

You can create a dashboard item based on standard reports already in Salesforce (meaning you don't even have to create a report first) or based on customized reports that you create.

37) C. The Record Owner, a User above the Record Owner, and the System Administrator.

The ability to see the "sharing" button on Account and Opportunity records depends on record ownership and user permissions. Here's the breakdown:

Can see the sharing button:

Record Owner: They always have access to sharing settings for the records they own.

System Administrator: They have full access to all data and can modify sharing settings for any record.

May or may not see the sharing button (depending on sharing settings):

User shared to the record: If a user is explicitly shared the record with "Read" or "Read/Write" access, they won't necessarily see the sharing button. The button typically appears only when the sharing model for the object is set to "Private" or "Public Read Only".

Cannot see the sharing button:

User above the Record Owner in the Role Hierarchy: While users above the record owner in the hierarchy can potentially access the record itself based on role permissions, they won't see the sharing button unless they are the record owner or a system administrator.

Therefore, the most accurate answer is:

C. The Record Owner, a User above the Record Owner, and the System Administrator.

Note: Even though users above the record owner might not see the sharing button, they might still be able to access the record based on sharing rules or other mechanisms.

Reference:

Manual sharesthe user may have gotten access through the Sharing button of the record. Only the record owner, an administrator, or a user above the owner in the role hierarchy can create or remove a manual share on the record.

https://help.salesforce.com/s/articleView?id=sf.faq_record_access.htm&type=5

38) A. They will not be able to complete the installation process as they have reached the maximum number of custom tabs.

Let's analyze the limitations and usage:

- **Professional Edition Limits:**
    - Custom Tabs: 10
    - Custom Objects: 40
    - Apps: 10
- **Current Usage:**
    - Custom Tabs: 7

- Custom Objects: 36
- Apps: 4

- **Expense Tracker Requirements:**
  - Custom Tabs: 4
  - Custom Objects: 3
  - Apps: 1

Adding the expense tracker will push the number of custom tabs over the limit (7 + 4 = 11).

Since Professional Edition has a limit of 10 custom tabs, the installation will fail due to exceeding this limit. The number of custom objects (36 + 3) and apps (4 + 1) would still be under the limits.

39) The best answer is:

A. The overall opportunity amount does not change but the converted amount in a report does.

Here's why:

Opportunity Currency: You created the opportunity with the currency set to British Pounds. This is the opportunity's base currency and represents the actual value of the deal.

Personal Currency: Your personal currency preference (British Pounds) doesn't affect the opportunity's base currency. It only impacts how you view the converted amount in reports or on the UI.

Currency Conversion Rate Update: The administrator updating the conversion rates only affects how Salesforce calculates the equivalent value in US Dollars (your default currency) for reporting or display purposes.

Essentially, the actual value of the opportunity in British Pounds remains the same, but the converted amount in US Dollars might change based on the updated conversion rate. Reports that display the opportunity value in US Dollars will reflect the new conversion rate.

The opportunity amounts won't change just because the conversion rate changes. The price in British Pounds is how much the product costs regardless of the exchange rate. The only reason the opportunity amount would change is if there was a discount applied, they had a coupon, you get the picture. The reason the amount in the report changes is because your company is based in the US, and you use USD as your currency, so any fluctuation in the exchange rate would cause the converted amount to change. The converted amount is what's being reflected in the report.

Example: Opportunity created for $50,000 EUR with an exchange rate of 1.25 = $44.247.79 USD. Change the exchange rate to 1.00 and the reported amount, and the actual amount, will then both be $50,000. Any future changes will only change the converted amount. The opportunity amount will always remain the same as long as no new items are added.

40) The most comprehensive answer for custom links in Salesforce is:

D. All of the Above

Custom links offer a versatile way to extend functionality within Salesforce. Here's how they can be used:

Launching an External URL: You can create a custom link that opens a specific website or web application outside of Salesforce.

Running an S Control: Custom links can be used to trigger S-Controls, which are pre-written JavaScript programs that execute specific actions within Salesforce. This allows you to automate tasks or perform actions that aren't readily available through standard buttons or functionalities.

Running a Report: Custom links can be configured to directly launch a specific report within Salesforce. This provides quick access to relevant data without navigating through menus.

41) A. True

Explanation: In Salesforce, you can manually share a record of a custom object with other users or groups to grant them access to the record. This can be done through the "Sharing" button on the record detail page.

You can manually share records of custom objects in Salesforce. Here's how:

Navigate to the Custom Object Record: Find the specific record you want to share.

Click the Sharing Button: Look for a button labeled "Sharing" or a similar icon. This button might be located on the detail page layout for the custom object.

Add Users or Groups: In the sharing settings window, you can search for and add specific users or groups who should have access to the record.

Set Access Level: Define the level of access you want to grant (e.g., Read, Read/Write).

Save: Once you've selected users/groups and set access levels, save the changes to apply the manual sharing settings.

Note: Sharing settings and permissions for custom objects can be more granular compared to standard objects. Make sure you have the necessary permissions to share the record.

42) B. False

Unfortunately, you cannot directly customize the related list for Opportunity Stage History on an Opportunity page layout. This functionality is not currently supported by Salesforce.

Here's what you can do:

View the Stage History: The Stage History related list is typically included by default on Opportunity page layouts. You can see the historical changes made to the opportunity stage within this related list.

Reports: You can create reports that track historical stage changes for opportunities. This might be a more flexible way to analyze the stage history data.

43) D. Sales Team is not typically a way to view a forecast in Salesforce.

Forecasts are typically viewed by:

Territory: This allows you to see the forecast for a specific geographic region.

Product Family: This allows you to see the forecast for a specific group of related products.

Date Range: This allows you to see the forecast for a specific period (e.g., month, quarter, year).

Sales teams themselves aren't a standard way to segment a forecast. However, forecasts might be assigned or owned by specific users within a sales team. You might be able to see forecasts associated with a particular user, but not directly by the entire sales team as a group.

Here are some ways forecasts might be associated with users:

Forecast Owner: Individual users can be assigned ownership of specific forecast territories or products. Viewing their forecasts would show the projections for their assigned areas.

Role Hierarchy: Depending on your role and permissions, you might be able to see forecasts owned by users below you in the role hierarchy.

Overall, while sales teams are a crucial part of the sales process, they aren't a direct way to filter or view forecasts in Salesforce.

A forecast type is a forecast that's configured to use a specific type of data: standard opportunity fields, opportunity splits, overlay splits, custom opportunity fields, product families, or territories. Each forecast type specifies a measurement: revenue or quantity. Territory, schedule date, and product date forecasts are available in Lightning Experience only.

44) Answer: C. Read, Create, Edit, and Delete permissions

Explanation: Profiles in Salesforce control the permissions and access levels for users, including the ability to read, create, edit, and delete records. Profiles do not control usernames, passwords, role level access, or sharing rules; these are managed through other means in Salesforce.

C. Read, Create, Edit, and Delete permissions: Profiles define the CRUD (Create, Read, Update, Delete) permissions that users have for various objects, fields, and functionalities within Salesforce. This determines what actions a user can perform on different data points.

Other Settings: Profiles can also control user interface settings, tab visibility, login IP ranges, and access to specific apps or features.

Not Controlled by Profiles:

A. Username and Password: These are managed separately during user creation and can't be directly modified through profiles.

B. Role level access: While profiles define permissions, role hierarchies determine which users have access to data owned by others. Roles control visibility and sharing, not the base-level permissions defined in profiles.

D. Sharing rules: Sharing rules are automated rules that define how records are shared with other users or groups based on specific criteria. They are separate from user profiles but can interact with profile-based permissions.

In essence, a profile acts as a blueprint that outlines a user's fundamental permissions and access within Salesforce.

45) A. True

When you convert a lead with a single marketing campaign in Salesforce, the campaign information does automatically map to the newly created contact and opportunity records (assuming you create an opportunity during conversion). This helps track the source of the lead and measure the effectiveness of your marketing campaigns.

Here's a breakdown of the process:

Lead with a Single Campaign: You have a lead record associated with a specific marketing campaign.

Lead Conversion: You initiate the lead conversion process.

Mapping Campaign Information: During conversion, Salesforce automatically maps the campaign information from the lead to the newly created contact and opportunity records (if created).

Tracking Results: This allows you to track which campaign generated the contact and potential sales opportunity. You can then analyze the effectiveness of your marketing efforts.

Note:

If the lead is associated with multiple campaigns, you'll typically have the option to choose which campaign to associate with the converted contact and opportunity during the conversion process.

Some configurations might require additional setup to ensure automatic campaign mapping during conversion.

46) A. True

Explanation: Related Lists in Salesforce display records from the "many" sides of a one-to-many relationship. They allow users to view and interact with related records that are linked to the record being viewed.

Related lists are a core feature in Salesforce used to display records associated with a parent record through one-to-many relationships. They provide a quick and convenient way to see child records without navigating away from the parent record.

Here's why related lists show the "many" sides:

One-to-Many Relationship: This type of relationship represents a scenario where one parent record can have many child records.

For example, an Account (parent) can have many Contacts (children) associated with it.

Related List Content: The related list on the Account page (parent) would display all the Contacts (children) linked to that specific Account. This showcases the "many" sides of the relationship, as a single Account can have multiple Contacts.

By displaying child records in a related list, users can easily access and manage them within the context of the parent record.

47) B. False

Explanation: Case Assignment Rules in Salesforce are not based on elapsed time but are instead used to automatically assign cases to users or queues based on criteria such as case attributes, user workload, or other conditions. Time-based triggers are typically handled by other Salesforce automation features like Workflow Rules or Process Builder.

Case Assignment Rules in Salesforce are not directly triggered by the time elapsed since the case was created. They are triggered based on the evaluation of specific criteria defined in the rule itself.

Here's a breakdown:

Case Assignment Rules: These are automation rules that define how cases are automatically assigned to specific queues or users based on pre-configured conditions. These conditions can involve various factors like the case subject, priority, or the type of product involved.

Time-Based Workflows: While case assignment rules aren't

directly time-based, Salesforce offers time-based workflows that can be used to automate actions based on the elapsed time since a record (including cases) was created or updated.

Alternatives for Time-Sensitive Case Routing:

Escalation Rules: These rules can be configured to reassign cases to different queues or users if they haven't been resolved within a specified timeframe. This can help ensure timely attention is given to urgent cases.

Workflows with Time Triggers: As mentioned earlier, workflows can be used to trigger actions based on time criteria. You could potentially create a workflow that triggers a notification or reassignment based on the case age.

48) Correct answer: AB

A. Sharing is inherited from parent.

B. Child needs to be manually deleted when parent is deleted.

Explanation:

A. In a Master/Detail relationship, sharing settings are inherited from the parent record, which means that the child record inherits the same sharing settings as its parent.

B. In a Master/Detail relationship, if the parent record is deleted, Salesforce automatically deletes the child records. This is known as a "cascade delete" behavior.

Master/Detail relationships in custom objects have the following characteristics:

A. Sharing is inherited from the parent: The child records inherit the sharing and security settings of the parent record.

B. Child needs to be manually deleted when parent is deleted: If the parent record is deleted, the child records are also deleted automatically.

Option C is incorrect. Both parent and child fields are available for reporting in a Master/Detail relationship.

Option D is incorrect. In a Master/Detail relationship, the child record is automatically deleted when the parent record is deleted, so it is not required.

49) The answer is:

A. True

When test driving an application on the Salesforce AppExchange Directory, you cannot view the S-Control configurations of that application.

Test drives are designed to provide a limited, read-only experience that showcases the core functionality and user interface of the application. Security measures prevent access to sensitive configurations like S-Controls, which are custom JavaScript programs that can potentially modify data or perform complex actions within Salesforce.

If you're interested in understanding the full capabilities of an application, including S-Control functionality, you might need to consult the application documentation or reach out to the app publisher for more information.

50) A. True

Explanation: Validation rules in Salesforce can evaluate fields on a child record (such as an opportunity line item) against fields on its parent record (such as the opportunity). This allows for validation of data consistency between related records.

Validation rules in Salesforce can assess an opportunity line item against the opportunity with which it's linked.

Validation rules are formulas that evaluate conditions based on field values within a record. They can be used to ensure data integrity and enforce specific business rules.

In the context of opportunities and opportunity line items, a validation rule could be created to:

- Check if the product on the line item is valid for the specific opportunity type.
- Verify if the total amount of all line items doesn't exceed the overall opportunity amount.
- Ensure specific fields on the opportunity line item are populated before saving the opportunity.

By leveraging validation rules, you can streamline your sales process and minimize the risk of errors in your opportunity data.

51) The answer is: B. False.

While there is a connection between profiles, applications, tabs, and objects, a lack of access to an application doesn't necessarily translate to a lack of access to the tabs and objects associated with it.

Here's a breakdown:

Profiles: Profiles define the base-level permissions users have within Salesforce. This includes CRUD (Create, Read, Update, Delete) access for various objects and fields.

Applications: Applications are bundles of functionalities, typically containing tabs and objects relevant to a specific area (e.g., Sales Cloud, Service Cloud).

Tabs and Objects: Tabs provide a way to organize and access objects within an application. Objects represent the core data entities within Salesforce (e.g., Accounts, Contacts, Opportunities).

Permissions Work Together:

Profile Permissions: A user's profile determines their overall object permissions. They can have Read, Create, Edit, or Delete access to specific objects regardless of the application they're associated with.

Application Access: While application access can simplify permission management by grouping related functionalities, it doesn't directly restrict access to the underlying objects.

Scenario:

Imagine a user has a profile with Read access to the Opportunity object but doesn't have access to the Sales Cloud application (which typically includes the Opportunity tab).

In this case, the user wouldn't see the Opportunity tab within the application interface.

However, they could still potentially access and view Opportunity records through other means (e.g., search, reports) since their profile grants them Read access to the Opportunity object itself.

Key Takeaway:

Profile permissions for objects are the core determinant of access, not necessarily the application that groups them. Applications primarily serve as a way to organize and present functionalities, but they don't directly control object-level permissions.

The Objects can be part of several different Apps, so not having access to an App that happens to contain (among other Objects), the Account Object would not mean you could not access the Account Object generally.

52) The field type that cannot be universally required in Salesforce is:

A. Lookup

Here's why:

Universal Requirement: This means a field is mandatory on all records, regardless of the record type or any other conditions.

Lookup Fields: These fields link a record to another record in Salesforce. Making a lookup field universally required could potentially prevent users from creating new records if there aren't any existing records to link to.

The other options (Text, Email, Number) can be universally required. This means you can make them mandatory fields that users must populate before saving a record, regardless of the record type.

53) B. URL that passes salesforce.com data like an organization's name is not possible within a Custom Web Tab.

Custom Web Tabs in Salesforce can include a URL, an S-Control, or an S-Control snippet. However, they cannot include a URL that passes Salesforce.com data like an organization's name.

While Custom Web Tabs can leverage merge fields within URLs to display some dynamic content based on Salesforce data, there are limitations. Merge fields typically work for user information or basic setup data, not necessarily the organization name itself.

Here's a breakdown:

Supported Merge Fields: Custom Web Tabs typically support merge fields for user information (e.g., User ID, Username) or basic setup data (e.g., Profile ID, Locale).

Organization Name: The organization name isn't readily available as a standard merge field within Custom Web Tabs. There might be workarounds or custom solutions to achieve this functionality, but it's not a native capability.

The other options (A. URL, C. S-Control snippet, and D. S-Control) are all valid inclusions within a Custom Web Tab with varying functionalities.

54) B. Account, Contact, or Opportunity.

Explanation: Custom lead fields in Salesforce can be mapped to Account, Contact, or Opportunity objects, allowing the data from lead records to be transferred to these related records when the lead is converted.

In Salesforce, when you convert a lead, you can map custom lead fields to corresponding fields in the newly created Account, Contact, and Opportunity records (assuming you create an Opportunity during conversion).

This mapping helps transfer relevant information about the lead to the associated account, contact, and potential sales opportunity.

Let's break down the other options:

A. Account, Contact, Opportunity, or Campaigns: While you can map lead fields to Accounts, Contacts, and Opportunities, campaigns are not directly involved in this specific mapping process.

C. Account or Contact Only: You can map lead fields to both Accounts and Contacts, or just Contacts or just Accounts depending on your needs. But Opportunity is also a valid option for mapping.

D. Contact or Opportunity Only: Similar to option C, you can choose to map to Contacts or Opportunities, but Accounts are also a possibility for lead field mapping.

55) Correct answer: ABD

A. Account

B. Contacts

D. Opportunities

Custom lead fields in Salesforce can be mapped to Account, Contact, and Opportunity objects during lead conversion. This mapping allows the data from lead fields to be transferred to these related objects when a lead is converted. However, custom lead fields cannot be mapped to Cases.

Lead Conversion: When you convert a qualified lead into a customer or potential sale, Salesforce allows you to map custom fields from the lead record to corresponding fields in the newly created related records.

Mapping Options: During the conversion process, you can choose to map a single custom lead field to an Account (representing the customer), a Contact (representing the individual within the customer organization), or an Opportunity (representing the potential sales deal).

Let's analyze the other option:

C. Cases: Cases are not directly involved in the lead conversion process. Custom lead fields typically map to Accounts, Contacts, or Opportunities to transfer relevant information about the lead to these related objects.

56) D. None of the above, the user cannot see the field at all

Explanation: Field Level Security in Salesforce controls the visibility of fields at the database level. If a field is hidden using Field Level Security, the user associated with that Profile cannot see the field in any context, including List Views, Reports, or Search results.

Field Level Security (FLS): When a field is hidden using FLS on a profile, it restricts user access to that field across various functionalities, including list views, reports, and search results.

While there might be some rare exceptions or configurations that could allow users to glimpse hidden fields, generally speaking, FLS is a powerful tool to enforce data visibility based on user permissions.

Let's explore the other options briefly:

A. List Views: If a list view includes the hidden field, users with the profile won't see that field in the list view.

B. Reports: Similar to list views, reports that include the hidden field won't display it for users with the profile.

C. Search: Search results won't return any information for the hidden field if a user with the profile searches for it.

Important Note:

There are some advanced configurations or tools (not typical Salesforce functionality) that might bypass FLS under specific circumstances. However, for the most part, FLS effectively restricts user access to hidden fields across various interfaces.

57) The answer is: B. False

While Salesforce supports relationships between various objects, there are limitations regarding how Person Accounts and Contacts interact:

Direct Relationship: A Person Account (representing an individual customer) cannot have a direct relationship with a Contact (representing another individual) on a Business Account (representing a company).

Here's a breakdown of the restrictions:

Person Account vs. Contact: Person Accounts are a special type of Account record that represents an individual, often used for business-to-consumer (B2C) interactions. Regular Contacts represent individual contacts typically associated with Business Accounts (companies).

Relationship Limitations: Due to the nature of these objects, Salesforce doesn't allow a direct lookup relationship between a Person Account and a Contact on a Business Account.

However, there are workarounds to achieve a similar outcome:

Contacts to Multiple Accounts: If your Salesforce edition supports it, you can enable the "Contacts to Multiple Accounts" feature. This allows a Contact (individual) to be linked to both a Person Account (representing their individual business) and a Business Account (representing the company they work for).

Custom Object: You could create a custom object to represent the relationship between the Person Account and the Business Account contact.

In essence, while a direct Person Account to Contact relationship on a Business Account isn't possible, there are alternative approaches to model similar scenarios in Salesforce.

58) C. Opportunity Amount multiplied by the probability.

Explanation: In Salesforce, the expected revenue in an opportunity is calculated by multiplying the Opportunity Amount by the Probability. The Probability represents the likelihood of winning the opportunity, and multiplying it by the amount gives an estimate of the expected revenue.

Opportunity Amount: This represents the total value (without considering discounts) associated with the opportunity.

Probability: This is a percentage value (typically between 0% and 100%) that reflects the likelihood of the opportunity closing successfully.

By multiplying the opportunity amount by the probability, you get a weighted value that represents the expected revenue from that opportunity. This takes into account both the potential deal size and the chance of it actually closing.

Let's break down the other options:

A. Amount multiplied by the total price of all opportunity line items: This wouldn't be entirely accurate. While the opportunity amount might be influenced by the total value of line items, it's not necessarily a direct multiplication. Opportunity amounts can be adjusted for various reasons.

B. The sales price on any line-item times the probability of the opportunity: This approach focuses on a single line item, which wouldn't necessarily reflect the overall value of the opportunity.

D. Amount multiplied by the discount percent: This calculation would result in a reduced value (discounted amount) and wouldn't represent the expected revenue, which considers the full potential value before discounts.

59) B. Leads, Accounts, Contacts, and Custom Objects.

Explanation: In Salesforce, a custom lookup field can be added to Leads, Accounts, Contacts, and Custom Objects to establish a relationship with a standard object. This allows you to link records from these standard objects to other custom or standard objects in Salesforce.

Custom Lookup Fields: These are special fields on custom objects that allow you to establish relationships with other Salesforce objects (standard or custom).

Supported Objects: You can create custom lookup fields on custom objects to reference standard objects like Leads, Accounts, Contacts, and even other custom objects within your Salesforce organization. This enables you to create connections and link related data points across different objects.

Let's analyze the other options:

A. Users and Custom Objects: Custom lookup fields cannot be used to directly link to Users objects. There are other ways to manage user relationships within Salesforce.

C. Users, Custom Objects and Campaigns: Similar to option A, custom lookup fields cannot link directly to Users objects. Campaigns can be related to other standard objects, but not necessarily through custom lookup fields on custom objects.

D. Custom Objects, Contract and Campaigns: Contracts are a standard object, but they typically wouldn't be the primary target for a custom lookup field on another custom object. While custom objects can have relationships with Campaigns, it might not be the most common use case for a custom lookup field.

By creating custom lookup fields that reference Leads, Accounts, Contacts, and other custom objects, you can create a rich network of interconnected data within your Salesforce instance.

60) The answer is: B. No

In Salesforce, if the Organization Wide Default sharing is set to private for all objects and no sharing rules have been created, users in the same role cannot view each other's data unless explicitly granted access through sharing settings or manual sharing.

Organization-Wide Defaults (OWD): When set to private for all objects, this is the most restrictive sharing setting. It prevents users from seeing any records they don't have explicit access to.

Sharing Rules: Since there are no sharing rules defined, there's no additional mechanism to override the restrictive OWD setting and grant access.

Sales Rep Role: While the role itself might not inherently restrict data visibility, in this scenario, the combination of a private OWD and no sharing rules creates a situation where users cannot see each other's data.

Default Sharing vs. User Permissions:

It's important to distinguish between OWD and user permissions:

OWD: Defines the baseline access level for all records of an object. In this case, private OWD is the starting point.

User Permissions: These determine what actions a user can perform on specific objects (e.g., Read, Create, Edit, Delete). Even if a user has Read permission on an object, the private OWD setting would still prevent them from seeing those records without additional sharing rules or manual sharing.

In essence, with a private OWD and no sharing rules, users are limited to seeing their own data and any records they've been granted access to through other sharing mechanisms.

With Private for all Objects and no Sharing Settings (Rules), viewing records you do not own is not possible unless s some other mechanism (Teams) is included.

Feel free to reach out to me anytime, and don't forget to connect with me on LinkedIn: <u>Georgio Daccache</u>. I'm always available to provide additional assistance and support.

GEORGIO DACCACHE

Good Luck

www.ingramcontent.com/pod-product-compliance
Lightning Source LLC
Chambersburg PA
CBHW052209220526
45471CB00004B/1892